RICHTHOFEN:
THE RED BARON IN OLD PHOTOGRAPHS

L. ARCHARD

AMBERLEY

Acknowledgements

My thanks to Phil Carradice, John Christopher and Campbell McCutcheon for permission to use images from their various collections in this book, and for their patience in answering my questions and queries. Other images come from the Library of Congress and from Flickr.

My thanks also go to Emily Brewer for all her patient help.

First published 2014

Amberley Publishing
The Hill, Stroud
Gloucestershire, GL5 4EP

www.amberley-books.com

British Library Cataloguing in Publication Data.
A catalogue record for this book is available from the British Library.

ISBN 978 1 4456 3348 0 (print)
ISBN 978 1 4456 3359 6 (ebook)

Typesetting and Origination by Amberley Publishing.
Printed in Great Britain.

Contents

Introduction

Manfred Freiherr von Richthofen, better known to posterity as the Red Baron, is probably the most famous fighter pilot that there has ever been. Born in 1892, he was a member of an aristocratic family from near Breslau in Silesia, which is now part of Poland. Von Richthofen seems to have been destined for military service from a young age, beginning his training as a cadet at the age of eleven. Following that, he became an officer in a regiment of Uhlans (lancers), and he was still in the cavalry when the First World War broke out. He saw service on the Eastern and Western fronts and seems to have joined the German flying service because the Western Front was settling into stalemate and he was bored; by his own admission, von Richthofen was a restless man.

Von Richthofen transformed into the Red Baron in early 1917. His career flying single-seat fighters had begun in September 1916, when he was recruited by another of the great German aces of the First World War, Oswald Boelcke, to join a special squadron of fighter pilots flying the new Albatros fighters. Prior to this, von Richthofen had served as an observer and later a pilot in two-seat aircraft. His first victory as a fighter pilot came on the first day that his squadron got their new Albatros aircraft, and to mark it, von Richthofen commissioned a jeweller to make a small silver cup engraved with the number one, the date and the type of aircraft he had shot down. After he had shot down sixteen aircraft, von Richthofen received the Ordre Pour le Mérite, otherwise known as the Blue Max, and was promoted to command a squadron in his own right, Jasta 11. 'Even in my dreams,' he would later write, 'I had never imagined that there would be a Richthofen's squadron of aeroplanes.' It was after von Richthofen took command of Jasta 11 that he became the Red Baron. As he himself put it, 'it occurred to me to have my packing case painted all over in staring red. The result was that everyone got to know my red bird. My opponents also seemed to have heard of the colour transformation.'

Later in the summer of 1917, Jasta 11 was combined with three other Jastas to create Jagdgeschwader (Fighter Squadron) 1, the famous Flying Circus, under von Richthofen's command. The nickname came from the brightly coloured aircraft flown by the pilots and their use of well-equipped trains with dining cars and sleeping compartments to travel between airfields. Like Boelcke, Richthofen would pick his own pilots for their skill and aggression, including his own brother Lothar, Ernst Udet (the second-highest-scoring German pilot of the war) and Herman Göring, part of whose appeal to the Nazis was that he was a hero to many Germans because of his service under von Richthofen's command.

On 6 July 1917, von Richthofen was wounded in the head by a bullet over Ypres. The wound and the concussion seem to have been enough to cause a change in his personality. Despite the seriousness of the wound, von Richthofen quickly discharged himself and returned to active duty. However, he would be grounded again over the winter of 1917/18 by structural problems with the new Fokker triplanes, with which his squadron had been equipped and sent on a propaganda tour.

On the night of 21 April 1918, von Richthofen and his squadron celebrated his eightieth victory. The next day, von Richthofen and some of his pilots, including his young and inexperienced cousin Wolfram, were involved in a dogfight with some Sopwith Camels of the RAF's No. 209 Squadron. An inexperienced Canadian pilot, Wilfred May, pursued Wolfram von Richthofen only to find himself pursued by Manfred. May's flight commander, Roy Brown, joined the dogfight; the three aircraft had flown over an Australian machine-gun unit in temporary trenches on the north bank of the Somme, and the Australians fired at the red triplane before it hit the ground. When they reached the wreckage, they found Manfred von Richthofen dead in his cockpit. Roy Brown claimed to have shot him down (although forensic analysis suggests it was a bullet from one of the Australian machine-gunners that hit Richthofen), and to commemorate the feat, the squadron crest still shows a falling red eagle.

A British aircraft dropped a message on von Richthofen's base at Cappy, bearing the tidings to his pilots. When the news reached Germany, the nation went into days of mourning. Von Richthofen himself was given a burial with full military honours by the nearest Allied flying unit, No. 3 Squadron of the Australian Flying Corps. He would later be exhumed and reburied in the Invalidenfriedhof, along with many other Prussian military heroes, in what would become East Berlin; von Richthofen's grave would practically be in the shadow of the Berlin Wall. He has since been reburied in the von Richthofen family plot at Wiesbaden, along with his mother and sister.

Manfred von Richthofen is still a presence in pop culture today, from Adrian Edmondson's portrayal in the classic episode of Blackadder Goes Forth to the Peanuts cartoons of Charles Schultz. Whenever a German aristocrat (often wearing a monocle) clambers into a red-painted fighter, ready to do battle, the Red Baron flies again. But what is his appeal today? It seems to be similar to that of Lawrence of Arabia: the idea that the single, glamorous, chivalrous individual still had a place in the vast, impersonal struggle that the First World War became, that despite everything there was space for honour and decency. Of course, that was von Richthofen the symbol, the man who became a legend in his own lifetime.

Von Richthofen himself was a man of many parts. He was a born hunter – he would write that his family had two hobbies, horse riding and hunting. Some of his habits, like the commissioning of those silver cups and his practice of collecting bits of wreckage from his victims, suggest a man who viewed aerial warfare as almost a field sport. From a military family, he had joined the cadets at the age of eleven and spent all his short life in the German armed forces. There are glimpses of a certain coldness in his autobiography, for instance when he talks about the treatment meted out to suspected *francs-tireurs*: 'Later on I heard that several days previously, the inhabitants had behaved very seditiously towards our cavalry, and later on towards our hospitals. It had therefore been found necessary to place quite a number of these gentlemen against the wall [i.e., they were executed by firing squad].' He respected the Allied pilots he shot down, visiting the wounded in hospital and bringing them presents and cigarettes. Hopefully, this book will serve as an introduction and encourage the reader to find out more about von Richthofen.

The photographs and drawings in this illustrated book are interspersed with text from von Richthofen's own autobiography, Der Rote Kampfflieger, which was written for propaganda purposes in 1917, when he was on leave following his head wound. It was translated into English in 1918 as The Red Battle Flier.

Manfred, Freiherr von Richthofen, the Red Baron. He is pictured here wearing the Iron Cross he won in September 1914 and the Ordre Pour le Mérite (better known as the Blue Max), which he was awarded in January 1917. (John Christopher Collection)

My Family

The members of my family – that of Richthofen – have taken no very great part in wars until now. The Richthofens have always lived in the country; indeed, there has scarcely been one of them without a landed estate, and the few who did not live in the country have, as a rule, entered the State service. My grandfather and all my ancestors before him had estates about Breslau and Striegau. Only in the generation of my grandfather did it happen that the first Richthofen, his cousin, became a General.

My mother belongs to the family Von Schickfuss und Neudorf. Their character resembles that of the Richthofen people. There were a few soldiers in that family. All the rest were agrarians. The brother of my great-grandfather Schickfuss fell in 1806. During the Revolution of 1848 one of the finest castles of a Schickfuss was burnt down. The Schickfuss have, as a rule, only become Captains of the Reserve.

In the family Schickfuss and in the family Falckenhausen – my grandmother's maiden name was Falckenhausen – there were two principal hobbies: horse riding and game shooting. My mother's brother, Alexander Schickfuss, has done a great deal of game shooting in Africa, Ceylon, Norway and Hungary.

My father is practically the first member of our branch of the family to become a professional soldier. At an early age he entered the Corps of Cadets and later joined the 12th Regiment of Uhlans. He was the most conscientious soldier imaginable. He began to suffer from difficulty of hearing and had to resign. He got ear trouble because he saved one of his men from drowning and though he was wet through and through he insisted upon continuing his duties as if nothing had happened, wet as he was, without taking notice of the rigour of the weather. The present generation of the Richthofens contains, of course, many more soldiers. In war every able-bodied Richthofen is, of course, on active service. In the very beginning of the present war I lost six cousins, and all were in the cavalry.

I was named after my uncle Manfred, who, in peacetime, was adjutant to His Majesty and Commander of the Corps of the Guards. During the war he has been Commander of a Corps of Cavalry.

My father was in the 1st Regiment of Cuirassiers in Breslau when I was born on 2 May 1892. We then lived at Kleinburg. I received tuition privately until my ninth year. Then I went for a year to school in Schweidnitz and then I became a Cadet in Wahlstatt. The people of Schwiednitz considered me as one of themselves.

Having been prepared for a military career as a Cadet, I entered the 1st Regiment of Uhlans.

My own adventures and experiences will be found in this book.

My brother, Lothar, is the other flying man called Richthofen. He wears the Ordre Pour le Mérite. My youngest brother is still in the Corps of Cadets and he is waiting anxiously until he is old enough to go on active service. My sister, like all the ladies of our family, is occupied in nursing the wounded.

Two images of Breslau; von Richthofen was born and grew up near the city. Then in the German region of Lower Silesia, it is now the Polish city of Wrocław. (Library of Congress)

My Life as a Cadet

As a little boy of eleven I entered the Cadet Corps. I was not particularly eager to become a Cadet, but my father wished it. So my wishes were not consulted.

I found it difficult to bear the strict discipline and to keep order. I did not care very much for the instruction I received. I never was good at learning things. I did just enough work to pass. In my opinion it would have been wrong to do more than was just sufficient, so I worked as little as possible. The consequence was that my teachers did not think overmuch of me. On the other hand, I was very fond of sport. Particularly I liked gymnastics, football, and other outdoor amusements. I could do all kinds of tricks on the horizontal bar. For this I received various prizes from the Commander.

I had a tremendous liking for all risky foolery. For instance, one fine day, with my friend Frankenberg, I climbed the famous steeple of Wahlstatt by means of the lightning conductor and tied my handkerchief to the top. I remember exactly how difficult it was to negotiate the gutters. Ten years later, when I visited my little brother at Wahlstatt, I saw my handkerchief still tied up, high in the air.

My friend Frankenberg was the first victim of the war as far as I know.

I liked very much better the Institution of Lichterfelde. I did not feel so isolated from the world and began to live a little more like a human being.

My happiest reminiscences of Lichterfelde are those of the great sports when my opponent was Prince Frederick Charles. The Prince gained many first prizes against me both in running and football, as I had not trained my body as perfectly as he had done.

I Enter the Army

Of course, I was very impatient to get into the Army. Immediately after passing my examination, I came forward and was placed in the 1st Regiment of Uhlans, 'Emperor Alexander III' [in spring 1911]. I had selected that regiment. It was garrisoned in my beloved Silesia and I had some acquaintances and relations there, who advised me to join it.

I had a colossal liking for the service with my regiment. It is the finest thing for a young soldier to be a cavalry man.

I can say only little about the time which I passed at the War Academy. My experience there reminds me too much of the Corps of Cadets and consequently my reminiscences are not over agreeable. At last I was given the epaulettes [in autumn 1912]. It was a glorious feeling, the finest I have ever experienced, when people called me Lieutenant.

German boys being trained for the army. 'I was not particularly eager to become a cadet, but my father wished it. So my wishes were not consulted.' (Library of Congress)

The military academy at Lichterfelde, just outside Berlin. (Wikipedia)

'My happiest reminiscences of Lichterfelde are those of the great sports when my opponent was Prince Frederick Charles.' A member of the Prussian royal house, the Hohenzollerns, the prince would win a bronze medal in equestrian team jumping at the 1912 Olympic Games in Stockholm. (Library of Congress)

Uhlans were originally Polish light cavalry (the team goes back to the eighteenth century), but the name was adopted by lancer regiments of the Russian, Austrian and Prussian armies. (Library of Congress)

The Uhlan regiment into which von Richthofen was commissioned when he became an officer was named for Tsar Alexander III. The close-knit nature of European royalty meant that many members of royal families held military rank, largely honorary, in other armies and navies.
Alexander was the father of the last tsar, Nicholas II, and brother-in-law to the British king, Edward VII. (Wikipedia)

The Outbreak of War

All the papers contained nothing but fantastic stories about the war. However, for several months we had been accustomed to war talk. We had so often packed our service trunks that the whole thing had become tedious. No one believed any longer that there would be war. We, who were close to the frontier, who were 'the eyes of the Army', to use the words of my Commander, believed least that there would be war.

On the day before military preparations began we were sitting with the people of the detached squadron at a distance of 10 kilometres from the frontier, in the officers' club. We were eating oysters, drinking champagne and gambling a little. We were very merry. No one thought of war.

It is true that, some days before, Wedel's mother had startled us a little. She had arrived from Pomerania in order to see her son before the beginning of the war. As she found us in the pleasantest mood and as she ascertained that we did not think of war, she felt morally compelled to invite us to a very decent luncheon.

We were extremely gay and noisy when suddenly the door opened. It disclosed Count Kospoth, the Administrator of Ols. He looked like a ghost.

We greeted our old friend with a loud 'Hoorah!' He explained to us the reason of his arrival. He had come personally to the frontier in order to convince himself whether the rumours of an impending world war were true. He assumed, quite correctly, that the best information could be obtained at the frontier. He was not a little surprised when he saw our peaceful assembly. We learned from him that all the bridges in Silesia were being patrolled by the military and that steps were being taken to fortify various positions.

We convinced him quickly that the possibility of war was absolutely nil and continued our festivity.

On the next day we were ordered to take the field.

German cavalry on the move at the start of the First World War. 'I rode at the head of a file of soldiers for the first time against the enemy at twelve o'clock midnight…' (J&C McCutcheon Collection)

A dramatic artist's impression of a force of Uhlans brought up short by a barbed-wire entanglement. 'We young cavalry Lieutenants had the most interesting task. We were to study the ground, to work towards the rear of the enemy, and to destroy important objects. All these tasks require real men.' (J&C McCutcheon Collection)

Opposite top: German officers entertaining. 'On the day before military preparations began … we were eating oysters, drinking champagne and gambling a little.' (Library of Congress)

Opposite bottom: Crowds in Berlin cheering the declaration of war. (J&C McCutcheon Collection)

We Cross the Frontier

To us cavalrymen on the frontier, the word 'war' had nothing unfamiliar. Every one of us knew to the smallest detail what to do and what to leave undone. At the same time, nobody had a very clear idea what the first thing would be. Every soldier was delighted to be able to show his capacity and his personal value.

We young cavalry Lieutenants had the most interesting task. We were to study the ground, to work towards the rear of the enemy, and to destroy important objects. All these tasks require real men.

Having in my pocket my directions and having convinced myself of their importance, through hard study during at least a year, I rode at the head of a file of soldiers for the first time against the enemy at twelve o'clock midnight.

A river marks the frontier and I expected to be fired upon on reaching it. To my astonishment, I could pass over the bridge without an incident. On the next morning, without having had any adventures, we reached the church tower of the village of Kieltze, which was well known to us through our frontier rides.

Everything had happened without seeing anything of the enemy, or rather without being seen by him. The question now was what should I do in order not to be noticed by the villagers? My first idea was to lock up the 'pope' [Russian priest]. We fetched him from his house, to his great surprise. I locked him up among the bells in the church tower, took away the ladder and left him sitting up above. I assured him that he would be executed if the population should show any hostile inclinations. A sentinel placed on the tower observed the neighbourhood.

I had to send reports every day by dispatch-riders. Very soon my small troop was converted entirely into dispatch-riders and dissolved, so that I had at last, as the only one remaining, to bring in my own report.

Up to the fifth night everything had been quiet. During that night the sentinel came suddenly rushing to the church tower, near which the horses had been put. He called out, 'The Cossacks are there!' The night was as dark as pitch. It rained a little. No stars were visible. One couldn't see a yard ahead.

As a precaution, we had previously breached the wall around the churchyard. Through the breach we took the horses into the open. The darkness was so great that we were in perfect security after having advanced 50 yards. I myself went with the sentinel, carbine in hand, to the place where he pretended he had seen Cossacks.

Gliding along the churchyard wall, I came to the street. When I got there I experienced a queer feeling, for the street swarmed with Cossacks. I looked over the wall, behind which the rascals had put the horses. Most of them had lanterns, and they acted very incautiously and were very loud. I estimated that there were from twenty to thirty of them. One had left his horse and gone to the pope, whom I had let off the day before.

Immediately it flashed through my brain: 'Of course we are betrayed!' Therefore, we had to be doubly careful. I could not risk a fight because I could not dispose of more than two carbines. Therefore, I resolved to play at robber and police.

After having rested a few hours, our visitors rode away again.

On the next day, I thought it wise to change our quarters. On the seventh day I was again back in my garrison and everyone stared at me as if I were a ghost. The staring was not due to my unshaved face, but because there had been a rumour that Wedel and I had fallen at Kalisch. The place where it had occurred, the time and all the circumstances of my death had been reported with such a wealth of detail that the report had spread throughout Silesia. My mother had already received visits of condolence. The only thing that had been omitted was an announcement of my death in the newspaper.

An amusing incident happened about the same time. A veterinary surgeon had been ordered to take ten Uhlans and to requisition horses on a farm. The farm was situated about 2 miles from the road. He came back full of excitement and reported to us:

> I was riding over a stubble field, the field where the scarecrows are, when I suddenly saw hostile infantry at a distance. Without a moment's hesitation I drew my sword and ordered the Uhlans to attack them with their lances. The men were delighted and at the fastest gallop they rushed across the field. When we came near the enemy I discovered that the hostile infantry consisted of some deer which were grazing in a nearby meadow. At that distance I had mistaken them for soldiers, owing to my short-sightedness.

For a long time that dear gentleman had to suffer the pleasantries of the rest of us because of his bold attack.

German cavalry raiders crossing a river using a small canvas boat. (J&C McCutcheon Collection)

Russian Cossack cavalry on parade. 'When I got there I experienced a strange feeling, for the street swarmed with Cossacks.' (Library of Congress)

A Russian church under occupation by German soldiers. Von Richthofen's Uhlans had their first encounter with the famous Russian Cossacks around a church just over the frontier. (Library of Congress)

To France

We were ordered to take the train in my garrison town. No one had any idea in what direction we were to go. There were many rumours but most of the talk was very wild. However, in this present case, we had the right idea: westward.

A second-class compartment had been given to four of us. We had to take in provisions for a long railway journey. Liquid refreshments, of course, were not lacking. However, already on the first day we discovered that a second-class compartment is altogether too narrow for four warlike youths. Therefore, we resolved to distribute ourselves. I arranged part of a luggage car and converted it into a bed/drawing room, to my great advantage. I had light, air, and plenty of space. I procured straw at one of the stations and put a tent cloth on top of it. In my improvised sleeping-car I slept as well as I did in my four-poster in Ostrowo. We travelled night and day, first through Silesia, and then through Saxony, going westward all the time. Apparently we were going in the direction of Metz. Even the train conductor did not know where he was going to. At every station, even at stations where we did not stop, there were huge crowds of men and women who bombarded us with cheers and flowers. The German nation had been seized by a wild war enthusiasm. That was evident. The Uhlans were particularly admired. The men in the train who had passed through the station before us had probably reported that we had met the enemy, and we had been at war only for a week. Besides, my regiment had been mentioned in the first official communiqué. The 1st Regiment of Uhlans and the 155th Regiment of Infantry had taken Kalisch. We were therefore celebrated as heroes and naturally felt like heroes. Wedel had found a Cossack sword which he showed to admiring girls. He made a great impression with it. Of course, we asserted that blood was sticking to it and we invented hair-raising tales about this peaceful sword of a police officer. We were very wild and merry until we were disembarked from the train at Busendorf, near Diedenhofen.

A short time before the train arrived we were held up in a long tunnel. It is uncomfortable enough to stop in a tunnel in peacetime, but to stop suddenly in war is still more uncomfortable. Some excited, high-spirited fellow wanted to play a joke and fired a shot. Before long there was general firing in the tunnel. It was surprising that no one was hurt. It has never been found out how the general shooting was brought about.

At Busendorf we had to get out of the train. The heat was so great that our horses almost collapsed. On the following day we marched unceasingly northward in the direction of Luxembourg. In the meantime, I had discovered that my brother had ridden in the same direction with a cavalry division a week before. I discovered his spoor once more, but I didn't see him until a year later.

Arrived in Luxembourg, no one knew what our relations were with the people of that little state. When I saw a Luxembourg prisoner, he told me that he would complain about me to the German Emperor if I did not set him free immediately. I thought there was reason in what he said. So I let him go. We passed through the town of Luxembourg and through Esch and we approached the first fortified towns of Belgium.

While advancing, our infantry, and indeed our whole division, manoeuvred exactly as in peacetime. All were extremely excited. It was a good thing that we had to act exactly as we had done at manoeuvres, otherwise we should certainly have done some wild things. To the right and to the left of us, before and behind us, on every road, marched troops belonging to different army corps. One had the feeling that everything was in a great disorder. Suddenly, this unspeakable cuddle-muddle was dissolved and became a most wonderfully arranged evolution.

I was entirely ignorant about the activities of our flying men, and I got tremendously excited whenever I saw an aviator. Of course I had not the slightest idea whether it was a German airman, or an enemy. I had at that time not even the knowledge that the German machines were marked with crosses and the enemy machines with circles. The consequence was that every aeroplane we saw was fired upon. Our old pilots are still telling of their painful feelings while being shot at by friend and enemy with perfect impartiality. We marched and marched, sending patrols far ahead, until we arrived at Arlon. I had an uneasy feeling when crossing, for a second time, an enemy frontier. Obscure reports of *francs-tireurs* had already come to my ears.

I had been ordered to work in connection with my cavalry division, acting as a connecting link. On that day I had ridden no less than 66 miles [probably km] with my men. Not a horse failed us. That was a splendid achievement. At Arlon I climbed the steeple in accordance with the tactical principles which we had been taught in peacetime. Of course, I saw nothing, for the wicked enemy was still far away. At that time we were very harmless. For instance, I had my men outside the town and had ridden alone on bicycle right through the town to the church tower and ascended it. When I came down again I was surrounded by a crowd of angry young men who made hostile eyes and who talked threateningly in undertones. My bicycle had, of course, been punctured and I had to go on foot for half an hour. This incident amused me. I should have been delighted had it come to a fight. I felt absolutely sure of myself with a pistol in my hand.

Later on I heard that several days previously, the inhabitants had behaved very seditiously towards our cavalry, and later on towards our hospitals. It had therefore been found necessary to place quite a number of these gentlemen against the wall. In the afternoon I reached the station to which I had been ordered, and learned that close to Arlon my only cousin Richthofen had been killed three days before. During the rest of the day I stayed with the cavalry division. During the night a causeless alarm took place, and late at night I reached my own regiment.

That was a beautiful time. We cavalrymen who had already been in touch with the enemy and had seen something of war were envied by the men of the other armies. For me it was the most beautiful time during the whole of the war. I would much like to pass again through the beginning of the war.

German cavalry making camp close to the Belgian frontier. After his ride across the frontier with the Russian empire, von Richthofen's unit was soon redeployed to the Western Front and advanced into Belgium. (J&C McCutcheon Collection)

Uhlans advancing through Belgium. Note the cart, which is being pulled by a dog, apparently a common practice in Belgium before the First World War. (J&C McCutcheon Collection)

An artist's impression, produced for the benefit of Allied audiences, showing Uhlans forcing Belgian civilians to taste their drinks to prove that they had not been poisoned. They also drank beer and wine, out of fear that the wells had been poisoned. (J&C McCutcheon Collection)

Ausflug
nach
Paris

Elsaß-
Lothringen
33644
6m

Auf Wiedersehn
auf dem
Boulevard

German hussars with two suspected Belgian *francs-tireurs*. German paranoia regarding Belgian and French civilians did not stop at poisoned beer; many civilians would be executed as suspected *francs-tireurs*, armed men dressed as civilians who fired on German troops. Von Richthofen mentions this happening more than once in the early days of the war. (Library of Congress)

Opposite top: A train full of German troops heading for the Western Front.

Opposite bottom: German troops advancing through Belgium. 'To the right and to the left of us, before and behind us, on every road, marched troops belonging to different army corps. One had the feeling that everything was in a great disorder.' The Schlieffen Plan called for most of the German army to attack through Belgium to knock out France as quickly as possible. (Library of Congress)

I Hear the Whistling of the First Bullets (21–22 August 1915)

I had been ordered to find out the strength of the enemy occupying the large forest near Virton. I started with fifteen Uhlans and said to myself, 'Today I shall have the first fight with the enemy.' But my task was not easy. In so big a forest there may be lots of things hidden which one cannot see.

I went to the top of a little hill. A few hundred paces in front of me was a huge forest extending over many thousands of acres. It was a beautiful August morning. The forest seemed so peaceful and still that I almost forgot all my warlike ideas.

We approached the margin of the forest. As we could not discover anything suspicious with our field glasses, we had to go near and find out whether we should be fired upon. The men in front were swallowed up by a forest lane. I followed and at my side was one of my best Uhlans. At the entrance to the forest was a lonely forester's cottage. We rode past it.

The soil indicated that a short time previously considerable numbers of hostile cavalry must have passed. I stopped my men, encouraged them by addressing a few words to them, and felt sure that I could absolutely rely upon every one of my soldiers. Of course, no one thought of anything except of attacking the enemy. It lies in the instinct of every German to rush at the enemy wherever he meets him, particularly if he meets hostile cavalry. In my mind's eye I saw myself at the head of my little troop sabring a hostile squadron, and was quite intoxicated with joyful expectation. The eyes of my Uhlans sparkled. Thus we followed the spoor at a rapid trot. After a sharp ride of an hour through the most beautiful mountain dale, the wood became thinner. We approached the exit. I felt convinced that there we should meet the enemy. Therefore, caution! To the right of our narrow path was a steep rocky wall many yards high. To the left, was a narrow rivulet and at the further side a meadow, 50 yards wide, surrounded by barbed wire. Suddenly, the trace of horses' hooves disappeared over a bridge into the bushes. My leading men stopped because the exit from the forest was blocked by a barricade.

Immediately I recognised that I had fallen into a trap. I saw a movement among the bushes behind the meadow at my left and noticed dismounted hostile cavalry. I estimated that there were fully 100 rifles. In that direction nothing could be done. My path right ahead was cut by the barricade. To the right were steep rocks. To the left the barbed wire surrounded the meadow and prevented me attacking as I had intended. Nothing was to be done except to go back. I knew that my dear Uhlans would be willing to do everything except to run away from the enemy. That spoilt our fun, for a second later we heard the first shot, which was followed by very intensive rifle fire from the wood. The distance was from 50 to 100 yards. I had told my men that they should join me immediately when they saw me lifting up my hand. I felt sure we had to go back. So I lifted my arm and beckoned my men to follow. Possibly, they misunderstood my gesture. The cavalrymen who were following me believed me in danger, and they came rushing along at a great speed to help me to get away. As we were on a narrow forest path, one can imagine the confusion which followed. There was a panic because the noise of every shot was increased tenfold by the narrowness of the path and the horses of the two men ahead rushed away. The last I saw of them was as they leaped the barricade. I never heard anything of them again. They were no doubt made prisoners. I myself turned my horse and gave him the spurs, probably for the first time during his life. I had the greatest difficulty to make the Uhlans who rushed towards me understand that they should not advance any further, that we were to turn round and get away. My orderly rode at my side. Suddenly his horse was hit and fell. I jumped over them and horses were rolling all around me. In short, it was a wild disorder. The last I saw of my servant, he was lying under his horse, apparently not wounded, but pinned down by the weight of the animal. The enemy had beautifully surprised us. He had probably observed us from the very beginning and had intended to trap us and to catch us unawares, as is the character of the French.

I was delighted when, two days later, I saw my servant standing before me. He wore only one boot for he had left the other one under the body of his horse. He told me how he had escaped. At least two squadrons of French cuirassiers had issued from the forest in order to plunder the fallen horses and the brave Uhlans. Not being wounded, he had jumped up, climbed the rocks and had fallen down exhausted among the bushes. About two hours later, when the enemy had again hidden himself, he had continued his flight. So he had joined me after some days, but he could tell me little about the fate of his comrades who had been left behind.

French dragoons, dismounted and manning a trench. 'Immediately I recognised that I had fallen into a trap. I saw a movement among the bushes behind the meadow at my left and noticed dismounted hostile cavalry.' (Library of Congress)

A patrol of French cavalry, a mixture of dragoons and chasseurs. (Library of Congress)

A Ride with Loen

The battle of Virton was proceeding. My comrade Loen and I had once more to ascertain what had become of the enemy. We rode after the enemy during the whole of the day, reached him at last and were able to write a very decent report. In the evening, the great question was: Shall we go on riding throughout the night in order to join our troops, or shall we economise our strength and take a rest so that we shall be fresh the next day? The splendid thing about cavalrymen on patrol is that they are given complete liberty of action.

We resolved to pass the night near the enemy and to ride on the next morning. According to our strategic notions, the enemy was retiring and we were following him. Consequently, we could pass the night with fair security.

Not far from the enemy there was a wonderful monastery with large stables. So both Loen and I had quarters for ourselves and our men. Of course, in the evening, when we entered our new domicile, the enemy was so near that he could have shot us through the windows.

The monks were extremely amiable. They gave us as much to eat and to drink as we cared to have and we had a very good time. The saddles were taken off the horses and they were very happy when for the first time in three days and three nights, a dead weight of nearly 300 lbs was taken from their backs. We settled down as if we were on manoeuvres and as if we were in the house of a delightful host and friend. At the same time, it should be observed that three days later, we hanged several of our hosts to the lanterns because they could not overcome their desire to take a hand in the war. But that evening they were really extremely amiable. We got into our nightshirts, jumped into bed, posted a sentinel, and let the Lord look after us.

In the middle of the night somebody suddenly flung open the door and shouted, 'Sir, the French are there!' I was too sleepy and too heavy to be able to reply. Loen, who was similarly incapacitated, gave the most intelligent answer: 'How many are they?' The soldier stammered, full of excitement, 'We have shot dead two, but we cannot say how many there are for it is pitch dark.' I heard Loen reply, in a sleepy tone, 'All right. When more arrive call me again.' Half a minute later both of us were snoring again.

The sun was already high in the heavens when we woke up from a refreshing sleep the next morning. We took an ample breakfast and then continued our journey.

As a matter of fact, the French had passed by our castle during the night and our sentinels had fired on them. As it was a very dark night nothing further followed.

Soon we passed through a pretty valley. We rode over the old battlefield of our division and discovered, to our surprise, that it was peopled not with German soldiers, but with French Red Cross men. Here and there were French soldiers. They looked as surprised at seeing us as we did at seeing them. Nobody thought of shooting. We cleared out as rapidly as possible and gradually it dawned upon us that our troops, instead of advancing, had retired. Fortunately, the enemy had retired at the same time in the opposite direction, otherwise I should now be somewhere in captivity.

We passed through the village of Robelmont where, on the previous day, we had seen our infantry in occupation. We encountered one of the inhabitants and asked him what had become of our soldiers. He looked very happy and assured me that the Germans had departed.

Late in the afternoon I reached my regiment and was quite satisfied with the course of events during the last twenty-four hours.

Uhlans charging into action. 'The cavalrymen who were following me believed me in danger, and they came rushing along at a great speed to help me to get away.' (J&C McCutcheon Collection)

'We rode over the old battlefield of our division and discovered, to our surprise, that it was peopled not with German soldiers, but with French Red Cross men. Here and there were French soldiers.' This photograph shows a unit of French soldiers taking a break to refresh themselves during a march. (Library of Congress)

Boredom Before Verdun

I am a restless spirit. Consequently, my activity in front of Verdun can only be described as boring. At the beginning I was in the trenches at a spot where nothing happened. Then I became a dispatch-bearer and hoped to have some adventures. But there I was mistaken. The fighting men immediately degraded me and considered me a base-hog. I was not really at the base but I was not allowed to advance further than 1,500 yards behind the front trenches. There, below the ground, I had a bombproof, heated habitation. Now and then I had to go to the front trenches. That meant great physical exertion, for one had to trudge uphill and downhill, criss-cross, through an unending number of trenches and mire-holes until at last one arrived at a place where men were firing. After having paid a short visit to the fighting men, my position seemed to me a very stupid one.

At that time the digging business was beginning. It had not yet become clear to us what it means to dig approaches and endless trenches. Of course, we knew the names of the various ditches and holes through the lessons which we had received at the Military Academy. However, the digging was considered to be the business of the military engineers. Other troops were supposed not to take a hand in it. Here, near Combres, everyone was digging industriously. Every soldier had a spade and a pick and took all imaginable trouble in order to get as deeply into the ground as possible. It was very strange that in many places the French were only 5 yards ahead of us. One could hear them speak and see them smoke cigarettes, and now and then they threw us a piece of paper. We conversed with them, but nevertheless, we tried to annoy them in every possible way, especially with hand grenades.

500 yards in front of us and 500 yards behind the trenches the dense forest of the Côte Lorraine had been cut down by the vast number of shells and bullets which were fired unceasingly. It seemed unbelievable that in front men could live. Nevertheless, the men in the front trenches were not in as bad a position as the men at the base.

After a morning visit to the front trenches, which usually took place at the earliest hours of the day, the more tedious business began. I had to attend to the telephone.

On days when I was off duty I indulged in my favourite pastime, game shooting. The forest of La Chaussée gave me ample opportunities. When going for a ride I had noticed that there were wild pigs about and I tried to find out where I could shoot them at night. Beautiful nights, with a full moon and snow, came to my aid. With the assistance of my servant, I built a shelter seat in a tree, at a spot where the pigs passed, and waited there at night. Thus I passed many a night sitting on the branch of a tree and on the next morning found that I had become an icicle. However, I got my reward. There was a sow which was particularly interesting. Every night she swam across the lake, broke into a potato field, always at the same spot, and then she swam back again. Of course I very much wished to improve my acquaintance with the animal. So I took a seat on the other shore of the lake. In accordance with our previous arrangement, Auntie Pig appeared at midnight for her supper. I shot her while she was still swimming and she would have been drowned had I not succeeded at the last moment in seizing her by the leg.

At another time, I was riding with my servant along a narrow path. Suddenly I saw several wild pigs crossing it. Immediately I jumped from the horse, grasped my servant's carbine and rushed several hundred yards ahead. At the end of the procession came a mighty boar. I had never yet seen such a beast and was surprised at its gigantic size. Now it ornaments my room and reminds me of my encounter.

In this manner I passed several months when, one fine day, our division became busy. We intended a small attack. I was delighted, for now at last I should be able to do something as a connecting link! But there came another disappointment! I was given quite a different job and now I had enough of it. I sent a letter to my Commanding General and evil tongues report that I told him, 'My dear Excellency! I have not gone to war in order to collect cheese and eggs, but for another purpose.' At first, the people above wanted to snarl at me. But then they fulfilled my wish. Thus I joined the Flying Service at the end of May 1915. My greatest wish was fulfilled.

Three German officers, rather more cheerful than von Richthofen described himself as being, looking out of the entrance to their dugout. (Library of Congress)

Opposite top: The French fortress city of Verdun prior to the First World War, in which it would play a major role as the target of a German offensive intended to inflict as many casualties as possible on the French. (Library of Congress)

Opposite bottom: German artillerymen taking a break while in the firing line at Verdun. 'My activity in front of Verdun can only be described as boring'. Verdun, with its forts, was a key French defensive position. (Library of Congress)

In the Air

The next morning at seven o'clock I was to fly for the first time as an observer! I was naturally very excited, for I had no idea what it would be like. Everyone whom I had asked about his feelings told me a different tale. The night before, I went to bed earlier than usual in order to be thoroughly refreshed the next morning. We drove over to the flying ground, and I got into a flying machine for the first time. The draught from the propeller was a beastly nuisance. I found it quite impossible to make myself understood by the pilot. Everything was carried away by the wind. If I took up a piece of paper, it disappeared. My safety helmet slid off. My muffler dropped off. My jacket was not sufficiently buttoned. In short, I felt very uncomfortable. Before I knew what was happening, the pilot went ahead at full speed and the machine started rolling. We went faster and faster. I clutched the sides of the car. Suddenly, the shaking was over, the machine was in the air and the earth dropped away from under me.

I had been told the name of the place to which we were to fly. I was to direct my pilot. At first we flew right ahead, then my pilot turned to the right, then to the left, but I had lost all sense of direction above our own aerodrome. I had not the slightest notion where I was! I began very cautiously to look over the side at the country. The men looked ridiculously small. The houses seemed to come out of a child's toy box. Everything seemed pretty. Cologne was in the background. The cathedral looked like a little toy. It was a glorious feeling to be so high above the earth, to be master of the air. I didn't care a bit where I was and I felt extremely sad when my pilot thought it was time to go down again. I should have liked best to start immediately on another flight. I have never had any trouble in the air such as vertigo. The celebrated American swings are to me disgusting. One does not feel secure in them, but in a flying machine one possesses a feeling of complete security. One sits in an aeroplane as in an easy chair. Vertigo is impossible. No man exists who has been turned giddy by flying. At the same time, flying affects one's nerves. When one races full speed through the air, and particularly when one goes down again, when the aeroplane suddenly dips, when the engine stops running, and when the tremendous noise is followed by an equally tremendous silence, then I would frantically clutch the sides and think that I was sure to fall to the ground. However, everything happened in such a matter-of-fact and natural way, and the landing, when we again touched terra firma, was so simple that I could not have such a feeling as fear. I was full of enthusiasm and should have liked to remain in an aeroplane all day long. I counted the hours to the time when we should start out again.

Etrich-Taube monoplanes, used by the German flying services. (J&C McCutcheon Collection)

Etrich-Taube monoplanes and biplanes. (J&C McCutcheon Collection)

Flanders from the air. 'I began very cautiously to look over the side at the country. The men looked ridiculously small. The houses seemed to come out of a child's toy box. Everything seemed pretty ... It was a glorious feeling to be so high above the earth, to be master of the air.' (J&C McCutcheon Collection)

As aerial reconnaissance began to develop, ways of camouflaging things so they could not be seen from the air were developed. This photograph shows an intelligence gathering post disguised under a haystack. (J&C McCutcheon Collection)

General Hoepner, commander of the German flying services, talking to a pilot who has just returned from a reconnaissance flight. (J&C McCutcheon Collection)

As an Observer with Mackensen

On 10 June 1915 I came to Grossenhain. Thence I was to be sent to the front. I was anxious to go forward as quickly as possible. I feared that I might come too late, that the world war might be over. I should have had to spend three months to become a pilot. By the time the three months had gone by, peace might have been concluded. Therefore, it never occurred to me to become a pilot. I imagined that, owing to my training as a cavalryman, I might do well as an observer. I was very happy when, after a fortnight's flying experience, I was sent out, especially as I was sent to the only spot where there was still a chance of a war, of movement: I was sent to Russia.

Mackensen was advancing gloriously. He had broken through the Russian position at Gorlice and I joined his army when we were taking Rawa Ruska. I spent a day at the aviation base and then I was sent to the celebrated 69th Squadron. Being quite a beginner, I felt very foolish. My pilot was a big gun, First Lieutenant Zeumer. He is now a cripple. Of the other men of the Section, I am the only survivor. Now came my most beautiful time. Life in the Flying Corps is very much like life in the cavalry. Every day, morning and afternoon, I had to fly and to reconnoitre, and I have brought back valuable information many a time.

With Holck in Russia (Summer 1915)

During June, July and August 1915, I remained with the Flying Squadron which participated in Mackensen's advance from Gorlice to Brest-Litovsk. I had joined it as quite a juvenile observer and had not the slightest idea of anything.

As a cavalryman, my business had consisted in reconnoitring. So the Aeroplane Service as an observer was in my line and it amused me vastly to take part in the gigantic reconnoitring flights which we undertook nearly every day.

For an observer it is important to find a pilot with a strong character. One fine day we were told, 'Count Holck will join us.' Immediately I thought, 'That is the man I want.'

Holck made his appearance, not as one would imagine, in a 60 hp Mercedes or in a first-class sleeping car. He came on foot. After travelling by railway for days and days, he had arrived in the vicinity of Jaroslav. Here he got out of the train for there was once more an unending stoppage. He told his servant to travel on with the luggage while he would go on foot. He marched along and after an hour's walking looked back, but the train did not follow him. So he walked and walked and walked without being overtaken by the train until, after a 30-mile walk, he arrived in Rawa Ruska, his objective. Twenty-four hours later, his orderly appeared with the luggage. His 30-mile walk proved no difficulty to that sportsman. His body was so well trained that he did not feel the tramp he had undertaken.

Count Holck was not only a sportsman on land. Flying also was to him a sport which gave him the greatest pleasure. He was a pilot of rare talent and particularity, and that is, after all, the principal thing. He towered head and shoulders above the enemy. We went on many a beautiful reconnoitring flight – I do not know how far – into Russia. Although Holck was so young, I had never a feeling of insecurity with him. On the contrary, he was always a support to me in critical moments. When I looked around and saw his determined face, I always had twice as much courage as I had had before.

My last flight with him nearly led to trouble. We had not had definite orders to fly. The glorious thing in the flying service is that one feels that one is a perfectly free man and one's own master as soon as one is up in the air.

We had to change our flying base and we were not quite certain in which meadow we were to land. In order not to expose our machine to too much risk in landing, we flew in the direction of Brest-Litovsk. The Russians were retiring everywhere. The whole countryside was burning. It was a terribly beautiful picture. We intended to ascertain the direction of the enemy columns, and in doing so flew over the burning town of Wicznice. A gigantic smoke cloud, which went up to about 6,000 feet, prevented us continuing our flight because we flew at an altitude of only 4,500 feet in order to see better. For a moment Holck reflected. I asked him what he intended to do and advised him to fly around the smoke cloud, which would have involved a round-about way of five minutes. Holck did not intend to do this. On the contrary. The greater the danger was, the more the thing attracted him. Therefore straight through! I enjoyed it, too, to be together with such a daring fellow. Our venturesomeness nearly cost us dear. As soon as the tail-end of the machine had disappeared in the smoke, the aeroplane began to reel. I could not see a thing for the smoke made my eyes water. The air was much warmer and beneath me I saw nothing but a huge sea of fire. Suddenly the machine lost its balance and fell, turning round and round. I managed to grasp a stay and hung on to it, otherwise I should have been thrown out of the machine. The first thing I did was to look at Holck and immediately I regained my courage for his face showed an iron confidence. The only thought which I had was, 'It is stupid, after all, to die so unnecessarily a hero's death.'

Later on, I asked Holck what had been his thoughts at the moment. He told me he had never experienced so unpleasant a feeling.

We fell down to an altitude of 1,500 feet above the burning town. Either through the skill of my pilot or by a Higher Will, perhaps by both, we suddenly dropped out of the smoke cloud. Our good Albatros found itself again and once more flew straight ahead as if nothing had happened.

We had now had enough of it and instead of going to a new base intended to return to our old quarter as quickly as possible. After all, we were still above the Russians and only at an altitude of 1,500 feet. Five minutes later I heard Holck, behind me, exclaiming, 'The motor is giving out.' I must add that Holck had not as much knowledge of motors as he had of horseflesh and I had not the slightest idea of mechanics. The only thing which I knew was that we should have to land among the Russians if the motor went on strike. So one peril had followed the other.

I convinced myself that the Russians beneath us were still marching with energy. I could see them quite clearly from our low altitude. Besides, it was not necessary to look, for the Russians shot at us with machine-guns with the utmost diligence. The firing sounded like chestnuts roasting near a fire.

Presently the motor stopped running altogether, for it had been hit. So we went lower and lower. We just managed to glide over a forest and landed at last in an abandoned artillery position which, the evening before, had still been occupied by Russians, as I had reported.

I told Holck my impressions. We jumped out of our box and tried to rush into the forest nearby, where we might have defended ourselves. I had with me a pistol and six cartridges. Holck had nothing.

When we had reached the wood we stopped and I saw with my glasses that a soldier was running towards our aeroplane. I was horrified to see that he wore not a spiked helmet but a cap. So I felt sure that it was a Russian. When the man came nearer Holck shouted with joy, for he was a Grenadier of the Prussian Guards. Our troops had once more stormed the position at the break of day and had broken through into the enemy batteries.

On that occasion Holck lost his little favourite, his doggie. He took the little animal with him on every flight. The dog would lie always quietly on Holck's fur in the fuselage. He was still with us when we were in the forest. Soon after, when we had talked with the Guardsman, German troops passed us. They were the staffs of the Guards and Prince Eitel Friedrich with his Adjutants and his Orderly Officers. The Prince supplied us with horses so that we two cavalrymen were sitting once more on oat-driven motors. Unfortunately doggie was lost while we were riding. Probably he followed other troops by mistake. Later in the evening we arrived in our old flying base on a cart. The machine was smashed.

An artist's impression of a German Taube monoplane being chased by rather eerie-looking anti-aircraft fire. (J&C McCutcheon Collection)

Kaiser Wilhelm (far left) with General von Mackensen (far right), commander of one of the German armies fighting the Russians on the Eastern Front. Von Richthofen's first squadron would be attached to von Mackensen's force. (Library of Congress)

The observer in a two-seat German aircraft poses with his machine gun. (J&C McCutcheon Collection)

Russian forces on the move. Although the Russians had advanced into Germany at the start of the war, and been defeated at the battle of Tannenberg, by the summer of 1915, when von Richthofen was serving with von Mackensen's forces, the Germans had advanced deep into the Russian Empire. (J&C McCutcheon Collection)

A camera typical of those used for aerial reconnaissance during the First World War. Using these unwieldy instruments would require both hands. (Library of Congress)

One use that was found for aircraft during the First World War was in spotting artillery, but not in the way you might think. As this large illustration shows, the aircraft would circle over the target and a man on the ground would use it as a marker to calculate the range for the gunners. (J&C McCutcheon Collection)

Top: Men of the German flying services on the Eastern Front: this German pilot and his companions are seen posing with a biplane that has been anchored to a tree somewhere in what had been the Russian province of Poland. (Library of Congress)

Above: An image of a two-seat German biplane starting on a reconnaissance flight. (J&C McCutcheon Collection)

Above: A German pilot and observer receiving their final instructions before they take off. (Library of Congress)

Right: Men of a German aerial reconnaissance unit receiving instructions from headquarters by telephone. (J&C McCutcheon Collection)

Russia–Ostend (From the Two-Seater to the Twin-Engined Fighter)

The German enterprise in Russia came gradually to a stop and suddenly I was transferred to a large battle-plane at Ostend on 21 August 1915. There I met an old acquaintance, friend Zeumer. Besides, I was attracted by the tempting name 'Large Battle-plane'.

I had a very good time during this part of my service. I saw little of the war but my experiences were invaluable to me, for I passed my apprenticeship as a battle-flier. We flew a great deal, we had rarely a fight in the air and we had no successes. We had seized a hotel on the Ostend shore, and there we bathed every afternoon. Unfortunately the only frequenters of the watering place were soldiers. Wrapped up in our many-coloured bathing gowns, we sat on the terraces of Ostend and drank our coffee in the afternoon.

One fine day we were sitting as usual on the shore drinking coffee. Suddenly we heard bugles. We were told that an English squadron was approaching. Of course, we did not allow ourselves to be alarmed and to be disturbed, but continued drinking our coffee. Suddenly, somebody called out, 'There they are!' Indeed, we could see on the horizon, though not very distinctly, some smoking funnels and later on could make out ships. Immediately we fetched our telescopes and observed them. There was, indeed, quite an imposing number of vessels. It was not quite clear to us what they intended to do, but soon we were to know better. We went up to the roof whence we could see more. Suddenly we heard a whistling in the air; then there came a big bang and a shell hit that part of the beach where a little before we had been bathing. I have never rushed as rapidly into the hero's cellar as I did at that moment. The English squadron shot perhaps three or four times at us and then it began bombarding the harbour and railway station. Of course, they hit nothing but they gave a terrible fright to the Belgians. One shell fell right in the beautiful Palace Hotel on the shore. That was the only damage that was done. Happily, they destroyed only English capital, for it belonged to Englishmen.

In the evening we flew again with energy. On one of our flights we had gone very far across the sea with our battle-plane. It had two motors and we were experimenting with a new steering gear which, we were told, would enable us to fly in a straight line with only a single motor working. When we were fairly far out I saw beneath us, not on the water but below the surface, a ship. It is a funny thing. If the sea is quiet, one can look down from above to the bottom of the sea. Of course it is not possible where the sea is 25 miles deep, but one can see clearly through several hundred yards of water. I had not made a mistake in believing that the ship was travelling not on the surface but below the surface. Yet it seemed at first that it was travelling above water. I drew Zeumer's attention to my discovery and we went lower in order to see more clearly. I am too little of a naval expert to say what it was but it was clear to me that it was bound to be a submarine. But of what nationality? That is a difficult question, which in my opinion can be solved only by a naval expert, and not always by him. One can scarcely distinguish colours under water and there is no flag. Besides, a submarine does not carry such things. We had with us a couple of bombs and I debated with myself whether I should throw them or not. The submarine had not seen us for it was partly submerged. We might have flown above it without danger and we might have waited until it found it necessary to come to the surface for air. Then we could have dropped our eggs. Herein lies, no doubt, a very critical point for our sister arm.

When we had fooled around the apparition beneath us for quite a while I suddenly noticed that the water was gradually disappearing from our cooling apparatus. I did not like that and I drew my colleague's attention to the fact. He pulled a long face and hastened to get home. However, we were approximately 12 miles from the shore and they had to be flown over. The motor began running more slowly and I was quietly preparing myself for a sudden cold immersion. But lo and behold, we got through! Our giant apple-barge barged along with a single motor and the new steering apparatus and we reached the shore and managed to land in the harbour without any special difficulty.

It is a good thing to be lucky. Had we not tried the new steering apparatus on that day there would not have been any hope for us. We should certainly have been drowned.

OSTEND – BATHERS IN RENTED GOWNS

German troops marching through Ostend. The city fell to the Germans in September 1914. (Library of Congress)

Opposite top: A party of bathers at Ostend, on the coast of Belgium. 'We had seized a hotel on the Ostend shore, and there we bathed every afternoon ... Wrapped up in our many-coloured bathing gowns, we sat on the terraces of Ostend and drank our coffee in the afternoon.' (Library of Congress)

Opposite bottom: The British fleet operating off the Ostend seafront. 'We were told that an English squadron was approaching ... There was, indeed, quite an imposing number of vessels ... The English squadron shot perhaps three or four times at us and then it began bombarding the harbour and railway station.' This image appears to be a montage, put together by the Bain News Service in the US for the benefit of American newspaper readers. (Library of Congress)

A Drop of Blood for the Fatherland

I have never been really wounded. At the critical moment I have probably bent my head or pulled in my chest. Often I have been surprised that they did not hit me. Once, a bullet went through both my fur-lined boots. Another time, a bullet went through my muffler. Another time one went along my arm through the fur and the leather jacket. But I have never been touched.

One fine day we started with our large battle-plane in order to delight the English with our bombs. We reached our object. The first bomb fell. It is very interesting to ascertain the effect of a bomb. At least one always likes to see it exploding. Unfortunately my large battle-plane, which was well qualified for carrying bombs, had a stupid peculiarity which prevented me from seeing the effect of a bomb-throw, for immediately after the throw the machine came between my eye and the object and covered it completely with its planes. This always made me wild because one does not like to be deprived of one's amusement. If you hear a bang down below and see the delightful greyish-whitish cloud of the explosion in the neighbourhood of the object aimed at, you are always very pleased. Therefore I waved to friend Zeumer that he should bend a little to the side. While waving to him I forgot that the infamous object on which I was travelling, my apple-barge, had two propellers which turned to the right and left of my observer seat. I meant to show him where approximately the bomb had hit, and bang! My finger was caught! I was somewhat surprised when I discovered that my little finger had been damaged. Zeumer did not notice anything.

Having been hit on the hand, I did not care to throw any more bombs. I quickly got rid of the lot and we hurried home. My love for the large battle-plane, which after all had not been very great, suffered seriously in consequence of my experience. I had to sit quiet for seven days and was debarred from flying. Only my beauty was slightly damaged, but after all, I can say with pride that I also have been wounded in the war.

During the first part of the First World War, the observer in an aircraft carrying bombs would have to literally throw them over the side as the racks needed to carry bombs below an aircraft had not yet been designed. (J&C McCutcheon Collection, Phil Carradice Collection)

My First Fight in the Air
(1 September 1915)

Zeumer and I were very anxious to have a fight in the air. Of course, we flew our large battle-plane. The title of our barge alone gave us so much courage that we thought it impossible for any opponent to escape us.

We flew every day from five to six hours without ever seeing an Englishman. I became quite discouraged, but one fine morning we again went out to hunt. Suddenly, I discovered a Farman aeroplane, which was reconnoitring without taking notice of us. My heart beat furiously when Zeumer flew towards it. I was curious to see what was going to happen. I had never witnessed a fight in the air and had about as vague an idea of it as it was possible to have.

Before I knew what was happening both the Englishman and I rushed by one another. I had fired four shots at most while the Englishman was suddenly in our rear firing into us like anything. I must say I never had any sense of danger because I had no idea how the final result of such a fight would come about. We turned and turned around one another until at last, to our great surprise, the Englishman turned away from us and flew off. I was greatly disappointed and so was my pilot.

Both of us were in very bad spirits when we reached home. He reproached me for having shot badly and I reproached him for not having enabled me to shoot well. In short, our aeroplane relations, which previously had been faultless, suffered severely. We looked at our machine and discovered that it had received quite a respectable number of hits. On the same day we went on the chase for a second time but again we had no success. I felt very sad. I had imagined that things would be very different in a battle squadron. I had always believed that one shot would cause the enemy to fall, but soon I became convinced that a flying machine can stand a great deal of punishment. Finally, I felt assured that I should never bring down a hostile aeroplane, however much shooting I did.

We did not lack courage. Zeumer was a wonderful flier and I was quite a good shot. We stood before a riddle. We were not the only ones to be puzzled. Many are nowadays in the same position in which we were then. After all, the flying business must really be thoroughly understood.

In the Champagne Battle

Our pleasant days at Ostend were soon past, for the Champagne battle began and we flew to the front in order to take part in it in our large battle-plane. Soon we discovered that our packing-case was a capacious aeroplane but that it could never be turned into a good battle-plane.

I flew once with Osteroth, who had a smaller flier than the apple-barge. About 3 miles behind the front we encountered a Farman two-seater. He allowed us to approach him and for the first time in my life I saw an aerial opponent from quite close by. Osteroth flew with great skill side by side with the enemy so that I could easily fire at him. Our opponent probably did not notice us, for only when I had trouble with my gun did he begin to shoot at us. When I had exhausted my supply of 100 bullets, I thought I could not trust my eyes when I suddenly noticed that my opponent was going down in curious spirals. I followed him with my eyes and tapped Osteroth's head to draw his attention. Our opponent fell and fell and dropped at last into a large crater. There he was, his machine standing on its head, the tail pointing towards the sky. According to the map he had fallen 3 miles behind the front. We had therefore brought him down on enemy ground. Otherwise I should have one more victory to my credit. I was very proud of my success. After all, the chief thing is to bring a fellow down. It does not matter at all whether one is credited for it or not.

A pilot's view of an artillery bombardment. (J&C McCutcheon Collection)

A squadron of cavalry can be seen moving across flat, open terrain between the wings of this aircraft. (J&C McCutcheon Collection)

An Allied artist's impression of air-to-air combat during the early part of the First World War. Initially, of course, aircraft did not have weapons fitted and crew members who wanted to defend themselves would have to carry a handgun, like the observer in this image, or a rifle. (J&C McCutcheon Collection)

How I Met Boelcke

Friend Zeumer got a Fokker monoplane. Therefore I had to sail through the world alone. The Champagne battle was raging. The French flying men were coming to the fore. We were to be combined in a battle squadron and took train on 1 October 1915.

In the dining car, at the table next to me, was sitting a young and insignificant-looking lieutenant. There was no reason to take any note of him except for the fact that he was the only man who had succeeded in shooting down a hostile flying man not once but four times. His name had been mentioned in the dispatches. I thought a great deal of him because of his experience. Although I had taken the greatest trouble, I had not brought an enemy down up to that time. At least I had not been credited with a success.

I would have liked so much to find out how Lieutenant Boelcke managed his business. So I asked him, 'Tell me, how do you manage it?' He seemed very amused and laughed, although I had asked him quite seriously. Then he replied, 'Well, it is quite simple. I fly close to my man, aim well and then of course he falls down.' I shook my head and told him that I did the same thing but my opponents unfortunately did not come down. The difference between him and I was that he flew a Fokker and I a large battle-plane.

I took great trouble to get more closely acquainted with that nice, modest fellow whom I badly wanted to teach me his business. We often played cards together, went for walks and I asked him questions. At last I formed a resolution that I also would learn to fly a Fokker. Perhaps then my chances would improve.

My whole aim and ambition became now concentrated upon learning how to manipulate the sticks myself. Hitherto I had been nothing but an observer. Happily, I soon found an opportunity to learn piloting on an old machine in the Champagne. I threw myself into the work with body and soul and after twenty-five training flights I stood before the examination in flying alone.

Another artist's impression of aerial combat, this time from the point of view of the observer, crouching over his machine gun and firing at a distant enemy aircraft. (J&C McCutcheon Collection)

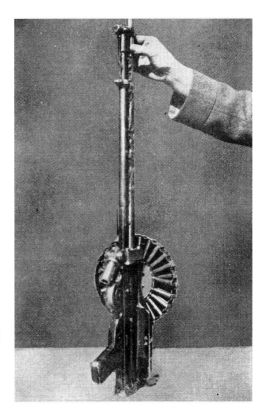

A German machine gun which fell into the Allied lines from the aircraft that had carried it. Interestingly, the original caption for the image refers to the weapon by its French name, *mitrailleuse*. (J&C McCutcheon Collection)

My First Solo Flight
(10 October 1915)

There are some moments in one's life which tickle one's nerves particularly and the first solo flight is among them.

One fine evening my teacher, Zeumer, told me, 'Now go and fly by yourself.' I must say, I felt like replying, 'I am afraid.' But this is a word which should never be used by a man who defends his country. Therefore, whether I liked it or not, I had to make the best of it and get into my machine.

Zeumer explained to me once more every movement in theory. I scarcely listened to his explanations for I was firmly convinced that I should forget half of what he was telling me.

I started the machine. The aeroplane went at the prescribed speed and I could not help noticing that I was actually flying. After all, I did not feel timorous but rather elated. I did not care for anything. I should not have been frightened no matter what happened. With contempt of death, I made a large curve to the left, stopped the machine near a tree, exactly where I had been ordered to, and looked forward to see what would happen. Now came the most difficult thing, the landing. I remembered exactly what movements I had to make. I acted mechanically and the machine moved quite differently from what I had expected. I lost my balance, made some wrong movements, stood on my head and succeeded in converting my aeroplane into a battered school bus. I was very sad, looked at the damage which I had done to the machine, which after all was not very great, and had to suffer from other people's jokes.

Two days later, I went with passion at the flying and suddenly I could handle the apparatus.

A fortnight later I had to take my first examination. Herr von T— was my examiner. I described the figure eight several times, exactly as I had been told to do, landed several times with success, in accordance with orders received, and felt very proud of my achievements. However, to my great surprise I was told that I had not passed. There was nothing to be done but to try once more to pass the initial examination.

My Training Time at Döberitz

In order to pass my examinations I had to go to Berlin. I made use of the opportunity to go to Berlin as observer in a giant plane. I was ordered to go by aeroplane to Döberitz, near Berlin, on 15 November 1915. In the beginning I took a great interest in the giant plane. But funnily enough, the gigantic machine made it clear to me that only the smallest aeroplane would be of any use for me in battle. A big aerial barge is too clumsy for fighting. Agility is needed and, after all, fighting is my business.

The difference between a large battle-plane and a giant-plane is that a giant-plane is considerably larger than a large battle-plane and that it is more suitable for use as a bomb-carrier than as a fighter.

I went through my examinations in Döberitz together with a dear fellow, First Lieutenant von Lyncker. We got on very well with one another and had the same inclinations and the same ideas as to our future activity. Our aim was to fly Fokkers and to be included in a battle squadron on the Western front. A year later we succeeded in working together for a short time. A deadly bullet hit my dear friend when bringing down his third aeroplane.

We passed many merry hours in Döberitz. One of the things which we had to do was to land in strange quarters. I used the opportunity to combine the necessary with the agreeable. My favourite landing place outside of our aerodrome was the Buchow Estate, where I was well known. I was there invited to shoot wild pigs. The matter could be combined only with difficulty with the service, for on fine evenings I wished both to fly and to shoot pigs. So I arranged for a place of landing in the neighbourhood of Buchow, whence I could easily reach my friends. I took with me a second pilot, who served as an observer, and sent him back in the evening. During the night I shot pigs and on the next morning was fetched by my pilot.

If I had not been fetched with the aeroplane I should have been in a hole for I should have had to march on foot a distance of about 6 miles. So I required a man who would fetch me in any weather. It is not easy to find a man who will fetch you under any circumstances.

Once, when I had passed the night trying to shoot pigs, a tremendous snowfall set in. One could not see 50 yards ahead. My pilot was to fetch me at eight sharp. I hoped that for once he would not come. But suddenly I heard a humming noise – one could not see a thing – and five minutes later my beloved bird was squatting before me on the ground. Unfortunately, some of his bones had got bent.

A German aviator starting off on his flight. 'There are some moments in one's life which tickle one's nerves particularly and the first solo flight is among them ... The aeroplane went at the prescribed speed and I could not help noticing that I was actually flying.' (Library of Congress)

A flying base outside Berlin. The flying school at Döberitz, outside the German capital, is where von Richthofen was formally trained as a pilot after having been taught by his friend Zeumer, and he made his first flight from here. (Library of Congress)

I Become a Pilot

On Christmas Day 1915, I passed my third examination. In connection with it I flew to Schwerin, where the Fokker works are situated, and had a look at them. As observer I took with me my mechanic, and from Schwerin I flew with him to Breslau, from Breslau to Schweidnitz, from thence to Luben and then returned to Berlin. During my tour I landed in lots of different places in between, visiting relatives and friends. Being a trained observer, I did not find it difficult to find my way.

In March 1916, I joined the Second Battle Squadron before Verdun and learned air fighting as a pilot. I learned how to handle a fighting aeroplane. I flew then a two-seater.

In the official communiqué of 26 April 1916, I am referred to for the first time, although my name is not mentioned. Only my deeds appear in it. I had had built into my machine a machine gun, which I had arranged very much in the way in which it is done in the Nieuport machines. I was very proud of my idea. People laughed at the way I had fitted it up because the whole thing looked very primitive. Of course I swore by my new arrangement and very soon I had an opportunity of ascertaining its practical value.

I encountered a hostile Nieuport machine, which was apparently guided by a man who also was a beginner, for he acted extremely foolishly. When I flew towards him, he ran away. Apparently he had trouble with his gun. I had no idea of fighting him but thought, 'What will happen if I now start shooting?' I flew after him, approached him as closely as possible and then began firing a short series of well-aimed shots with my machine gun. The Nieuport reared up in the air and turned over and over.

At first both my observer and I believed that this was one of the numerous tricks which French fliers habitually indulge in. However, his tricks did not cease. Turning over and over, the machine went lower and lower. At last my observer patted me on the head and called out to me, 'I congratulate you. He is falling.' As a matter of fact, he fell into a forest behind Fort Douaumont and disappeared among the trees. It became clear to me that I had shot him down, but on the other side of the front. I flew home and reported merely, 'I had an aerial fight and have shot down a Nieuport.' The next day I read of my action in the official communiqué. Of course I was very proud of my success, but that Nieuport does not figure among the fifty-two aeroplanes which I have brought down.

The communiqué of 26 April stated, 'Two hostile flying machines have been shot down by aerial fighting above Fleury, south and west of Douaumont.'

A group of German pilots posing on their airfield in eastern France in front of one of their aircraft. 'In March 1916, I joined the Second Battle Squadron before Verdun and learned air fighting as a pilot. I learned how to handle a fighting aeroplane. I flew then a two-seater.' (Library of Congress)

A captured Nieuport fighter, painted in German markings. The first aircraft von Richthofen shot down as a pilot was a Nieuport, although it was not numbered among his final total of eighty because it fell on the Allied side of the lines and could not be confirmed. (J&C McCutcheon Collection)

At the end of April 1916, Holck, von Richthofen's pilot from when he was flying as an observer on the Eastern Front, was shot down and killed near Verdun. In his autobiography, von Richthofen takes a rather blasé attitude to the perils of combat flying at the time of the First World War, but there must have been a lot of danger; Holck's fate would probably have been commonplace, although more so for inexperienced pilots. (Library of Congress)

A captured Caudron aircraft, painted in German markings. Richthofen describes Holck as having been shot down in a fight with three Caudrons over Verdun's Fort Douaumont. (Library of Congress)

Holck's Death (30 April 1916)

As a young pilot I once flew over Fort Douaumont at a moment when it was exposed to a violent drumfire. I noticed that a German Fokker was attacking three Caudron machines. It was my misfortune that a strong west wind was blowing. That was not favourable to me. The Fokker was driven over the town of Verdun in the course of the fight. I drew the attention of my observer to the struggle. He thought that the German fighting man must be a very smart fellow. We wondered whether it could be Boelcke and intended to inquire when we came down. Suddenly, I saw to my horror that the German machine, which previously had attacked, had fallen back upon the defensive. The strength of the French fighting men had been increased to at least ten and their combined assaults forced the German machine to go lower and lower.

I could not fly to the German's aid. I was too far away from the battle. Besides, my heavy machine could not overcome the strong wind against me. The Fokker fought with despair. His opponents had rushed him down to an altitude of only about 1,800 feet. Suddenly, he was once more attacked by his opponents and he disappeared, plunging into a small cloud. I breathed more easily, for in my opinion the cloud had saved him.

When I arrived at the aerodrome, I reported what I had seen and was told that the Fokker man was Count Holck, my old comrade in the Eastern Theatre of war. Count Holck had dropped straight down, shot through the head. His death deeply affected me for he was my model. I tried to imitate his energy and he was a man among men also as a character.

I Fly in a Thunderstorm

Our activity before Verdun was disturbed in the summer of 1916 by frequent thunderstorms. Nothing is more disagreeable for flying men than to have to go through a thunderstorm. In the Battle of the Somme a whole English flying squadron came down behind our lines and became prisoners of war because they had been surprised by a thunderstorm.

I had never yet made an attempt to get through thunder clouds but I could not suppress my desire to make the experiment. During the whole day thunder was in the air. From my base at Mont, I had flown over to the fortress of Metz nearby in order to look after various things. During my return journey I had an adventure.

I was at the aerodrome of Metz and intended to return to my own quarters. When I pulled my machine out of the hangar the first signs of an approaching thunderstorm became noticeable. Clouds which looked like a gigantic pitch-black wall approached from the north. Old, experienced pilots urged me not to fly. However, I had promised to return and I should have considered myself a coward if I had failed to come back because of a silly thunderstorm. Therefore I meant to try.

When I started the rain began falling. I had to throw away my goggles otherwise I should not have seen anything. The trouble was that I had to travel over the mountains of the Moselle, where the thunderstorm was just raging. I said to myself that probably I should be lucky and get through and rapidly approached the black cloud which reached down to the earth. I flew at the lowest possible altitude. I was compelled absolutely to leap over houses and trees with my machine. Very soon I knew no longer where I was. The gale seized my machine as if it were a piece of paper and drove it along. My heart sank within me. I could not land among the hills. I was compelled to go on.

I was surrounded by an inky blackness. Beneath me the trees bent down in the gale. Suddenly I saw right in front of me a wooded height. I could not avoid it. My Albatros managed to take it. I was able to fly only in a straight line. Therefore I had to take every obstacle that I encountered. My flight became a jumping competition, purely and simply. I had to jump over trees, villages, spires and steeples, for I had to keep within a few yards of the ground, otherwise I should have seen nothing at all. The lightning was playing around me. At that time I did not yet know that lightning cannot touch flying machines. I felt certain of my death for it seemed to me inevitable that the gale would throw me at any moment into a village or a forest. Had the motor stopped working, I should have been done for.

Suddenly, I saw that on the horizon the darkness had become less thick. Over there the thunderstorm had passed. I would be saved if I were able to get so far. Concentrating all my energy, I steered towards the light. Suddenly I got out of the thunder-cloud. The rain was still falling in torrents. Still, I felt saved. In pouring rain I landed at my aerodrome. Everyone was waiting for me, for Metz had reported my start and had told them that I had been swallowed up by a thunder cloud. I shall never again fly through a thunderstorm unless the Fatherland should demand this.

Now, when I look back, I realise that it was all very beautiful. Notwithstanding the danger during my flight, I experienced glorious moments which I would not care to have missed.

My First Time in a Fokker

From the beginning of my career as a pilot I had only a single ambition, the ambition to fly in a single-seater battle-plane. After worrying my commander for a long time I at last obtained permission to mount a Fokker. The revolving motor was a novelty to me. Besides, it was a strange feeling to be quite alone during the flight.

The Fokker belonged jointly to a friend of mine who has died long ago, and to myself. I flew in the morning and he in the afternoon. Both he and I were afraid that the other fellow would smash the box. On the second day, we flew towards the enemy. When I flew in the morning no Frenchman was to be seen. In the afternoon it was his turn. He started but did not return. There was no news from him.

Late in the evening the infantry reported an aerial battle between a Nieuport and a German Fokker, in the course of which the German machine had apparently landed at the Mort Homme. Evidently the occupant was friend Reimann, for all the other flying men had returned. We regretted the fate of our brave comrade. Suddenly, in the middle of the night, we heard over the telephone that a German flying officer had made an unexpected appearance in the front trenches at the Mort Homme. It appeared that this was Reimann. His motor had been smashed by a shot. He had been forced to land. As he was not able to reach our own lines, he had come to the ground in No Man's Land. He had rapidly set fire to the machine and had then quickly hidden himself in a mine crater. During the night he had slunk into our trenches. Thus ended our joint enterprise with a Fokker.

A few days later I was given another Fokker. This time I felt under a moral obligation to attend to its destruction myself. I was flying for the third time. When starting, the motor suddenly stopped working. I had to land right away in a field and in a moment the beautiful machine was converted into a mass of scrap metal. It was a miracle that I was not hurt.

The Fokker Eindecker was designed by the Dutch engineer Anthony Fokker and helped German pilots establish a period of superiority over the Allied air services known as the Fokker Scourge. Oswald Boelcke would score nineteen of his forty victories flying an Eindecker. (Flickr/ San Diego Air and Space Museum, J&C McCutcheon Collection)

Bombing in Russia

In June we were suddenly ordered to entrain. No one knew where we were going, but we had an idea and we were not over much surprised when our Commander told us that we were going to Russia. We had travelled through the whole of Germany with our perambulating hotel, which consisted of dining and sleeping cars, and arrived at last at Kovel. There we remained in our railway cars. There are many advantages in dwelling in a train. One is always ready to travel on and need not change one's quarters.

In the heat of the Russian summer a sleeping car is the most horrible instrument of martyrdom imaginable. Therefore, I agreed with some friends of mine, Gerstenberg and Scheele, to take quarters in the forest nearby. We erected a tent and lived like gypsies. We had a lovely time.

In Russia our battle squadron did a great deal of bomb throwing. Our occupation consisted of annoying the Russians. We dropped our eggs on their finest railway establishments. One day our whole squadron went out to bomb a very important railway station. The place was called Manjewicze and was situated about 20 miles behind the front. That was not very far. The Russians had planned an attack and the station was absolutely crammed with colossal trains. Trains stood close to one another. Miles of rails were covered with them. One could easily see that from above. There was an object for bombing that was worthwhile.

One can become enthusiastic over anything. For a time I was delighted with bomb throwing. It gave me a tremendous pleasure to bomb those fellows from above. Frequently, I took part in two expeditions on a single day. On the day mentioned, our object was Manjewicze. Everything was ready. The aeroplanes were ready to start. Every pilot tried his motor, for it is a painful thing to be forced to land against one's will on the wrong side of the front line, especially in Russia. The Russians hated the flyers. If they caught a flying man they would certainly kill him. That is the only risk one ran in Russia for the Russians had no aviators, or practically none. If a Russian flying man turned up he was sure to have bad luck and would be shot down. The anti-aircraft guns used by Russia were sometimes quite good, but they were too few in number. Compared with flying in the West, flying in the East is absolutely a holiday.

The aeroplanes rolled heavily to the starting point. They carried bombs to the very limit of their capacity. Sometimes, I dragged 300 lbs of bombs with a normal C-machine. Besides, I had with me a very heavy observer, who apparently had not suffered in any way from the food scarcity. I had also with me a couple of machine guns. I was never able to make proper use of them in Russia. It is a pity that my collection of trophies contains not a single Russian.

Flying with a heavy machine which is carrying a great dead weight is no fun, especially during the midday summer heat in Russia. The barges sway in a very disagreeable manner. Of course, heavily laden though they are, they do not fall down. The 150 hp motors prevent it. At the same time it is no pleasant sensation to carry such a large quantity of explosives and benzine.

At last we get into a quiet atmosphere. Now comes the enjoyment of bombing. It is splendid to be able to fly in a straight line and to have a definite object and definite orders. After having thrown one's bombs, one has the feeling that he has achieved something, while frequently, after searching for an enemy to give battle to, one comes home with a sense of failure at not having brought a hostile machine to the ground. Then a man is apt to say to himself, 'You have acted stupidly.'

It gave me a good deal of pleasure to throw bombs. After a while my observer learned how to fly perpendicularly over the objects to be bombed and to make use of the right moment for laying his egg with the assistance of his aiming telescope.

The run to Manjewicze is very pleasant and I have made it repeatedly. We passed over gigantic forests which were probably inhabited by elks and lynxes. But the villages looked miserable. The only substantial village in the whole neighbourhood was Manjewicze. It was surrounded by innumerable tents, and countless barracks had been run up near the railway station. We could not make out the Red Cross.

Another flying squadron had visited the place before us. That could be told by the smoking houses and barracks. They had not done badly. The exit of the station had obviously been blocked by a lucky hit. The engine was still steaming. The engine driver had probably dived into a shelter. On the other side of the station an engine was just coming out. Of course I felt tempted to hit it. We flew towards the engine and dropped a bomb a few hundred yards in front of it. We had the desired result. The engine stopped. We turned and continued throwing bomb after bomb on the station, carefully taking aim through our aiming telescope. We had plenty of time, for nobody interfered with us. It is true that an enemy aerodrome was in the neighbourhood but there was no trace of hostile pilots. A few anti-aircraft guns were busy, but they shot not in our direction but in another one. We reserved a bomb, hoping to make particularly good use of it on our way home.

Suddenly, we noticed an enemy flying machine starting from its hangar. The question was whether it would attack us. I did not believe in an attack. It was more likely that the flying man was seeking security in the air, for when bombing machines are about, the air is the safest place.

We went home by roundabout ways and looked for camps. It was particularly amusing to pepper the gentlemen down below with machine guns. Half-savage tribes from Asia are even more startled when fired at from above than are cultured Englishmen. It is particularly interesting to shoot at hostile cavalry. An aerial attack upsets them completely. Suddenly the lot of them rush away in all directions of the compass. I should not like to be the Commander of a Squadron of Cossacks which has been fired at with machine guns from aeroplanes.

By and by we could recognise the German lines. We had to dispose of our last bomb and we resolved to make a present of it to a Russian observation balloon, the only observation balloon they possessed. We could quite comfortably descend to within a few hundred yards of the ground in order to attack it. At first, the Russians began to haul it in very rapidly. When the bomb had been dropped the hauling stopped. I did not believe that I had hit it. I rather imagined that the Russians had left their chief in the air and had run away. At last we reached our front and our trenches and were surprised to find when we got home that we had been shot at from below. At least one of the planes had a hole in it.

Another time, and in the same neighbourhood, we were ordered to meet an attack of the Russians, who intended to cross the River Stokhod. We came to the danger spot laden with bombs and carrying a large number of cartridges for our machine guns. On arrival at the Stokhod, we were surprised to see that hostile cavalry was already crossing. They were passing over a single bridge. Immediately it was clear to us that one might do a tremendous lot of harm to the enemy by hitting the bridge.

Dense masses of men were crossing. We went as low as possible and could clearly see the hostile cavalry crossing by way of the bridge with great rapidity. The first bomb fell near the bridge. The second and third followed immediately. They created a tremendous disorder. The bridge had not been hit. Nevertheless traffic across it had completely ceased. Men and animals were rushing away in all directions. We had thrown only three bombs but the success had been excellent. Besides, a whole squadron of aeroplanes was following us. Lastly, we could do other things. My observer fired energetically into the crowd down below with his machine gun and we enjoyed it tremendously. Of course, I cannot say what real success we had. The Russians have not told us. Still, I imagined that I alone had caused the Russian attack to fail. Perhaps the official account of the Russian War Office will give me details after the war.

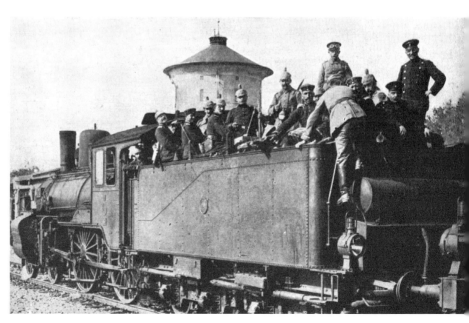

German troops crowd the tender of the locomotive of a train heading eastwards. In June 1916, von Richthofen's squadron was ordered to move to the Eastern Front. (J&C McCutcheon Collection)

Left: A German soldier loading a bomb on to an early bomb rack. (Library of Congress)

Below: A rather romanticised artist's impression of Cossacks crossing a river. 'It was particularly amusing to pepper the gentlemen down below with machine guns. Half-savage tribes from Asia are even more startled when fired at from above than are cultured Englishmen.' Western observers often saw the Tsar's conscript army as something 'other', hence both von Richthofen's comment and the rumours that regularly spread through Britain of Russian troops landing in Scotland with snow still on their boots. (J&C McCutcheon Collection)

This page:
Top: The Russian aviation pioneer and aircraft designer Igor Sikorski, standing in front of one of his creations at the start of the First World War. 'The only risk one ran in Russia, for the Russians had no aviators, or practically none. If a Russian flying man turned up he was sure to have bad luck and would be shot down.' (J&C McCutcheon Collection)

Bottom: A bombed bridge, seen from the air. 'On arrival at the Stokhod, we were surprised to see that hostile cavalry was already crossing. They were passing over a single bridge. Immediately it was clear to us that one might do a tremendous lot of harm to the enemy by hitting the bridge.' Although von Richthofen attacked, he did not have as much success as the pilot who hit this bridge. (J&C McCutcheon Collection)

These two German postcards, originally printed in colour, are an idealised representation of bombing missions on the Eastern Front. (J&C McCutcheon Collection)

At Last

The August sun was almost unbearably hot on the sandy flying ground at Kovel. While we were chatting among ourselves, one of my comrades said, 'Today the great Boelcke arrives on a visit to us, or rather to his brother!' In the evening the great man came to hand. He was vastly admired by all and he told us many interesting things about his journey to Turkey. He was just returning from Turkey and was on the way to Headquarters. He imagined that he would go to the Somme to continue his work. He was to organise a fighting squadron. He was empowered to select from the flying corps those men who seemed to him particularly qualified for his purpose.

I did not dare to ask him to be taken on. I did not feel bored by the fighting in Russia. On the contrary, we made extensive and interesting flights. We bombed the Russians at their stations. Still, the idea of fighting again on the Western Front attracted me. There is nothing finer for a young cavalry officer than the chase of the air. The next morning, Boelcke was to leave us. Quite early, somebody knocked at my door and before me stood the great man with the Ordre Pour le Mérite. I knew him, as I have previously mentioned, but still I had never imagined that he would come to look me up in order to ask me to become his pupil. I almost fell upon his neck when he inquired whether I cared to go with him to the Somme. Three days later, I sat in the railway train and travelled through the whole of Germany, straight away to the new field of my activity. At last my greatest wish was fulfilled. From now onwards began the finest time of my life. At that time I did not dare to hope that I should be as successful as I have been. When I left my quarters in the East, a good friend of mine called out after me, 'See that you do not come back without the Ordre Pour le Mérite.'

Oswald Boelcke. 'He was vastly admired by all ... He imagined that he would go to the Somme to continue his work. He was to organise a fighting squadron. He was empowered to select from the flying corps those men who seemed to him particularly qualified for his purpose.' (Library of Congress)

My First English Victim

We were all at the butts trying our machine guns. On the previous day we had received our new aeroplanes and the next morning Boelcke was to fly with us. We were all beginners. None of us had had a success so far. Consequently, everything that Boelcke told us was to us Gospel truth. Every day, during the last few days, he had, as he said, shot one or two Englishmen for breakfast.

The next morning, 17 September, was a gloriously fine day. It was therefore only to be expected that the English would be very active. Before we started, Boelcke repeated to us his instructions and for the first time we flew as a squadron, commanded by the great man whom we followed blindly.

We had just arrived at the front when we recognised a hostile flying squadron that was proceeding in the direction of Cambrai. Boelcke was of course the first to see it, for he saw a great deal more than ordinary mortals. Soon we understood the position and every one of us strove to follow Boelcke closely. It was clear to all of us that we should pass our first examination under the eyes of our beloved leader.

Slowly, we approached the hostile squadron. It could not escape us. We had intercepted it, for we were between the front and our opponents. If they wished to go back they had to pass us. We counted the hostile machines. They were seven in number. We were only five. All the Englishmen flew large, bomb-carrying two-seaters. In a few seconds the dance would begin.

Boelcke had come very near the first English machine but he did not yet shoot. I followed. Close to me were my comrades. The Englishman nearest to me was travelling in a large boat painted with dark colours. I did not reflect very long but took my aim and shot. He also fired and so did I, and both of us missed our aim. A struggle began and the great point for me was to get to the rear of the fellow because I could only shoot forward with my gun. He was differently placed for his machine gun was movable. It could fire in all directions.

Apparently he was no beginner, for he knew exactly that his last hour had arrived at the moment when I got at the back of him. At that time I had not yet the conviction 'He must fall!' which I have now on such occasions, but on the contrary, I was curious to see whether he would fall. There is a great difference between the two feelings. When one has shot down one's first, second or third opponent, then one begins to find out how the trick is done.

My Englishman twisted and turned, going criss-cross. I did not think for a moment that the hostile squadron contained other Englishmen who conceivably might come to the aid of their comrade. I was animated by a single thought: 'The man in front of me must come down, whatever happens.' At last a favourable moment arrived. My opponent had apparently lost sight of me. Instead of twisting and turning, he flew straight along. In a fraction of a second I was at his back with my excellent machine. I gave a short series of shots with my machine gun. I had gone so close that I was afraid I might dash into the Englishman. Suddenly, I nearly yelled with joy for the propeller of the enemy machine had stopped turning; I had shot his engine to pieces. The enemy was compelled to land, for it was impossible for him to reach his own lines. The English machine was curiously swinging to and fro. Probably something had happened to the pilot. The observer was no longer visible. His machine gun was apparently deserted. Obviously I had hit the observer and he had fallen from his seat.

The Englishman landed close to the flying ground of one of our squadrons. I was so excited that I landed also and my eagerness was so great that I nearly smashed up my machine. The English flying machine and my own stood close together. I rushed to the English machine and saw that a lot of soldiers were running towards my enemy. When I arrived I discovered that my assumption had been correct. I had shot the engine to pieces and both the pilot and observer were severely wounded. The observer died at once and the pilot while being transported to the nearest dressing station. I honoured the fallen enemy by placing a stone on his beautiful grave.

When I came home, Boelcke and my other comrades were already at breakfast. They were surprised that I had not turned up. I reported proudly that I had shot down an Englishman. All were full of joy for I was not the only victor. As usual, Boelcke had shot down an opponent for breakfast and every one of the other men also had downed an enemy for the first time.

I would mention that since that time no English squadron ventured as far as Cambrai as long as Boelcke's squadron was there.

This image is captioned as being a German Albatros. When the Boelcke squadron was formed, the pilots all flew Albatros D.I fighters, except for Boelcke himself, who was provided with a D.II. (Library of Congress)

An artist's impression of a pilot and observer greeting and saluting the crew of the aircraft which they have just shot down. Von Richthofen treated many of the crews he shot down with great courtesy, visiting them in hospital (and bringing cigarettes and presents) and even arranging for a gravestone for one who died. (J&C McCutcheon Collection)

A similar attitude could be found on the other side of the lines. This photograph shows the French ace Vedrines standing between the two crew members of a German Aviatik aircraft, which he had just shot down. (J&C McCutcheon Collection)

The Battle of the Somme

During my whole life I have not found a happier hunting ground than in the course of the Battle of the Somme. In the morning, as soon as I had got up, the first Englishmen arrived, and the last did not disappear until long after sunset. Boelcke once said that this was the El Dorado of the flying men.

There was a time when, within two months, Boelcke's bag of machines increased from twenty to forty. We beginners had not at that time the experience of our master and we were quite satisfied when we did not get a hiding. It was an exciting period. Every time we went up, we had a fight. Frequently we fought really big battles in the air. There were sometimes from forty to sixty English machines, but unfortunately the Germans were often in the minority. With them quality was more important than quantity.

Still, the Englishman is a smart fellow. That we must allow. Sometimes the English came down to a very low altitude and visited Boelcke in his quarters, upon which they threw their bombs. They absolutely challenged us to battle and never refused fighting.

We had a delightful time with our chasing squadron. The spirit of our leader animated all his pupils. We trusted him blindly. There was no possibility that one of us would be left behind. Such a thought was incomprehensible to us. Animated by that spirit, we gaily diminished the number of our enemies.

On the day when Boelcke fell, the squadron had brought down forty opponents. By now the number has been increased by more than 100. Boelcke's spirit lives still among his capable successors.

Boelcke's Death

One day we were flying, once more guided by Boelcke against the enemy. We always had a wonderful feeling of security when he was with us. After all, he was the one and only. The weather was very gusty and there were many clouds. There were no aeroplanes about except fighting ones.

From a long distance we saw two impertinent Englishmen in the air who actually seemed to enjoy the terrible weather. We were six and they were two. If they had been twenty and if Boelcke had given us the signal to attack, we should not have been at all surprised.

The struggle began in the usual way. Boelcke tackled the one and I the other. I had to let go because one of the German machines got in my way. I looked around and noticed Boelcke settling his victim about 200 yards away from me. It was the usual thing. Boelcke would shoot down his opponent and I had to look on. Close to Boelcke flew a good friend of his. It was an interesting struggle. Both men were shooting. It was probable that the Englishman would fall at any moment. Suddenly, I noticed an unnatural movement of the two German flying machines. Immediately, I thought: collision. I had not yet seen a collision in the air. I had imagined that it would look quite different. In reality, what happened was not a collision. The two machines merely touched one another. However, if two machines go at the tremendous pace of flying machines, the slightest contact has the effect of a violent concussion.

Boelcke drew away from his victim and descended in large curves. He did not seem to be falling, but when I saw him descending below me I noticed that part of his plane had broken off. I could not see what happened afterwards, but in the clouds he lost an entire plane. Now his machine was no longer steerable. It fell, accompanied all the time by Boelcke's faithful friend.

When we reached home, we found the report 'Boelcke is dead!' had already arrived. We could scarcely realise it.

The greatest pain was, of course, felt by the man who had the misfortune to be involved in the accident.

It is a strange thing that everybody who met Boelcke imagined that he alone was his true friend. I have made the acquaintance of about forty men, each of whom imagined that he alone was Boelcke's intimate. Each imagined that he had the monopoly of Boelcke's affections. Men whose names were unknown to Boelcke believed that he was particularly fond of them. This is a curious phenomenon which I have never noticed in anyone else. Boelcke had not a personal enemy. He was equally polite to everybody, making no differences.

The only one who was perhaps more intimate with him than the others was the very man who had the misfortune to be in the accident which caused his death. Nothing happens without God's will. That is the only consolation which any of us can put to our souls during this war.

A stylised artist's impression of an Allied aircraft returning across the lines from a patrol. The Allied air services constantly patrolled in an effort to support ground forces at the Somme, which von Richthofen described as the happiest hunting ground of his life. (J&C McCutcheon Collection)

An action-packed artist's impression of ground strafing, an aircraft using its machine guns to attack enemy troops. (J&C McCutcheon Collection)

Opposite page: Wrecked Allied aircraft. 'While I was fighting my opponent, Immelmann had tackled another Englishman and had brought him down in the same locality. Both of us flew quickly home in order to have a look at the machines we had downed ... I arrived in the vicinity of my victim. In the meantime, a lot of people had of course gathered around.' (Library of Congress, J&C McCutcheon Collection)

My Eighth Victim

In Boelcke's time eight was quite a respectable number. Those who hear nowadays of the colossal bags made by certain aviators must feel convinced that it has become easier to shoot down a machine. I can assure those who hold that opinion that the flying business is becoming more difficult from month to month, and even from week to week. Of course, with the increasing number of aeroplanes one gains increased opportunities for shooting down one's enemies, but at the same time, the possibility of being shot down oneself increases. The armament of our enemies is steadily improving and their number is increasing. When Immelmann shot down his first victim, he had the good fortune to find an opponent who carried not even a machine gun. Such little innocents one finds nowadays only at the training ground for beginners.

On 9 November 1916, I flew towards the enemy with my little comrade Immelmann, who then was eighteen years old. We both were in Boelcke's squadron of chasing aeroplanes. We had previously met one another and had got on very well. Comradeship is a most important thing. We went to work. I had already bagged seven enemies and Immelmann five. At that time this was quite a lot.

Soon after our arrival at the front, we saw a squadron of bombing aeroplanes. They were coming along with impertinent assurance. They arrived in enormous numbers, as was usual during the Somme Battle. I think there were about forty or fifty machines approaching. I cannot give the exact number. They had selected an object for their bombs not far from our aerodrome. I reached them when they had almost attained their objective. I approached the last machine. My first few shots incapacitated the hostile machine-gunner. Possibly they had tickled the pilot, too. At any rate, he resolved to land with his bombs. I fired a few more shots to accelerate his progress downwards. He fell close to our flying ground at Lagnicourt.

While I was fighting my opponent, Immelmann had tackled another Englishman and had brought him down in the same locality. Both of us flew quickly home in order to have a look at the machines we had downed. We jumped into a motor car, drove in the direction where our victims lay and had to run along a distance through the fields. It was very hot, therefore I unbuttoned all my garments, even the collar and the shirt. I took off my jacket and left my cap in the car but took with me a big stick. My boots were miry up to the knees. I looked like a tramp. I arrived in the vicinity of my victim. In the meantime, a lot of people had of course gathered around.

At one spot there was a group of officers. I approached them, greeted them, and asked the first one whom I met whether he could tell me anything about the aspect of the aerial battle. It is always interesting to find out how a fight in the air looks to the people down below. I was told that the English machines had thrown bombs and that the aeroplane that had come down was still carrying its bombs.

The officer who gave me this information took my arm, went with me to the other officers, asked my name and introduced me to them. I did not like it, for my attire was rather disarranged. On the other hand, all the officers looked as spick and span as on parade. I was introduced to a personage who impressed me rather strangely. I noticed a General's trousers, an Order at the neck, an unusually youthful face and undefinable epaulettes. In short, the personage seemed extraordinary to me. During our conversation I buttoned my shirt and collar and adopted a somewhat military attitude.

I had no idea who the officer was. I took my leave and went home again. In the evening, the telephone rang and I was told that the undefinable somebody with whom I had been talking had been His Royal Highness, the Grand Duke of Saxe-Coburg-Gotha. I was ordered to go to him. It was known that the English had intended to throw bombs on his headquarters. Apparently, I had helped to keep the aggressors away from him. Therefore I was given the Saxe-Coburg-Gotha medal for bravery. I always enjoy this adventure when I look at the medal.

Left: A photograph showing a First World War dogfight. (J&C McCutcheon Collection)

Below: Max Immelmann was the first German flying ace of the First World War, and the first aviator to win the Ordre Pour le Mérite, receiving his medal at the same ceremony at which Boelcke had been decorated. (Phil Carradice Collection)

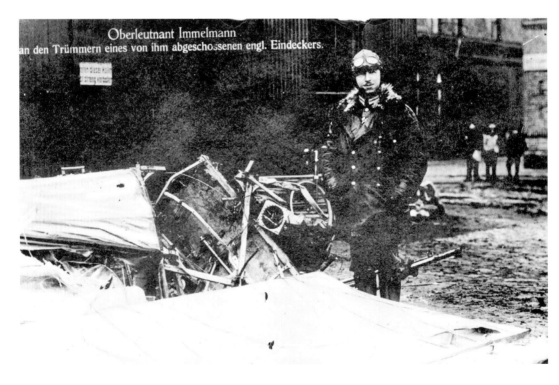

Oberleutnant Immelmann an den Trümmern eines von ihm abgeschossenen engl. Eindeckers.

Major Hawker

I was extremely proud when, one fine day, I was informed that the airman whom I had brought down on 23 November 1916 was the English Immelmann.

In view of the character of our fight, it was clear to me that I had been tackling a flying champion. One day I was blithely flying to give chase when I noticed three Englishmen who also had apparently gone a-hunting. I noticed that they were ogling me and as I felt much inclination to have a fight, I did not want to disappoint them.

I was flying at a lower altitude. Consequently, I had to wait until one of my English friends tried to drop on me. After a short while, one of the three came sailing along and attempted to tackle me in the rear. After firing five shots he had to stop, for I had swerved in a sharp curve.

The Englishman tried to catch me up in the rear while I tried to get behind him. So we circled round and round like madmen after one another at an altitude of about 10,000 feet.

First we circled twenty times to the left, and then thirty times to the right. Each tried to get behind and above the other. Soon I discovered that I was not meeting a beginner. He had not the slightest intention of breaking off the fight. He was travelling in a machine which turned beautifully. However, my own was better at rising than his, and I succeeded at last in getting above and beyond my English waltzing partner.

When we had got down to about 6,000 feet without having achieved anything in particular, my opponent ought to have discovered that it was time for him to take his leave. The wind was favourable to me, for it drove us more and more towards the German position. At last we were above Bapaume, about half a mile behind the German front. The impertinent fellow was full of cheek and when we had got down to about 3,000 feet he merrily waved to me as if he would say, 'Well, how do you do?'

The circles which we made around one another were so narrow that their diameter was probably no more than 250 or 300 feet. I had time to take a good look at my opponent. I looked down into his carriage and could see every movement of his head. If he had not had his cap on, I would have noticed what kind of a face he was making.

My Englishman was a good sportsman, but by and by the thing became a little too hot for him. He had to decide whether he would land on German ground or whether he would fly back to the English lines. Of course, he tried the latter, after having endeavoured in vain to escape me by looping and suchlike tricks. At that time his first bullets were flying around me, for hitherto neither of us had been able to do any shooting.

When he had come down to about 300 feet he tried to escape by flying in a zigzag course during which, as is well known, it is difficult for an observer to shoot. That was my most favourable moment. I followed him at an altitude of from 250 feet to 150 feet, firing all the time. The Englishman could not help falling. But the jamming of my gun nearly robbed me of my success.

My opponent fell, shot through the head, 150 feet behind our line. His machine gun was dug out of the ground and it ornaments the entrance of my dwelling.

The Duke of Saxe-Coburg-Gotha. 'I was told that the indefinable somebody with whom I had been talking had been His Royal Highness, the Grand Duke of Saxe-Coburg-Gotha ... It was known that the English had intended to throw bombs on his headquarters. Apparently, I had helped to keep the aggressors away from him. Therefore I was given the Saxe-Coburg-Gotha medal for bravery. I always enjoy this adventure when I look at the medal.'

Lanoe Hawker, in a photograph published to mark his decoration with the DSO (Distinguished Service Order) for attacking the zeppelin shed at Gontrode in Belgium using hand grenades. By the time he faced von Richthofen, Hawker had also won the Victoria Cross. (J&C McCutcheon Collection)

I Get the Ordre Pour le Mérite

I had brought down my sixteenth victim, and I had come to the head of the list of all the flying chasers. I had obtained the aim which I had set myself. In the previous year my friend Lynker, with whom I was training, had asked me, 'What is your object? What will you obtain by flying?' I replied, jokingly, 'I would like to be the first of the chasers. That must be very fine.' That I should succeed in this I did not believe myself. Other people also did not expect my success. Boelcke is supposed to have said, not to me personally – I have only heard the report – when asked, 'Which of the fellows is likely to become a good chaser?', 'That is the man!', pointing his finger in my direction.

Boelcke and Immelman were given the Ordre Pour le Mérite when they had brought down their eighth aeroplane. I had downed twice that number. The question was, what would happen to me? I was very curious. It was rumoured that I was to be given command of a chasing squadron.

One fine day a telegram arrived, which stated, 'Lieutenant von Richthofen is appointed Commander of the Eleventh Chasing Squadron.'

I must say I was annoyed. I had learnt to work so well with my comrades of Boelcke's squadron and now I had to begin all over again, working hand in hand with different people. It was a beastly nuisance. Besides, I should have preferred the Ordre Pour le Mérite.

Two days later, when we were sitting sociably together, we men of Boelcke's squadron, celebrating my departure, a telegram from Headquarters arrived. It stated that His Majesty had graciously condescended to give me the Ordre Pour le Mérite. Of course, my joy was tremendous.

I had never imagined that it would be so delightful to command a chasing squadron. Even in my dreams, I had not imagined that there would ever be a Richthofen's squadron of aeroplanes.

Le Petit Rouge

It occurred to me to have my packing case painted all over in staring red. The result was that everyone got to know my red bird. My opponents also seemed to have heard of the colour transformation.

During a fight on quite a different section of the front, I had the good fortune to shoot into a Vickers two-seater which peacefully photographed the German artillery position. My friend, the photographer, had not the time to defend himself. He had to make haste to get down upon firm ground, for his machine began to give suspicious indications of fire. When we airmen notice that phenomenon in an enemy plane, we say, 'He stinks!' As it turned out it was really so. When the machine was coming to earth, it burst into flames.

I felt some human pity for my opponent and had resolved not to cause him to fall down but merely to compel him to land. I did so particularly because I had the impression that my opponent was wounded, for he did not fire a single shot.

When I had got down to an altitude of about 1,500 feet, engine trouble compelled me to land without making any curves. The result was very comical. My enemy with his burning machine landed smoothly while I, his victor, came down next to him in the barbed wire of our trenches and my machine overturned.

The two Englishmen, who were not a little surprised at my collapse, greeted me like sportsmen. As mentioned before, they had not fired a shot and they could not understand why I had landed so clumsily. They were the first two Englishmen whom I had brought down alive. Consequently, it gave me particular pleasure to talk to them. I asked them whether they had previously seen my machine in the air, and one of them replied, 'Oh, yes. I know your machine very well. We call it "Le Petit Rouge".'

When he fought against von Richthofen, Hawker was flying a DH2 aircraft. (Wikipedia)

Kaiser Wilhelm decorating aviators. 'A telegram from Headquarters arrived. It stated that His Majesty had graciously condescended to give me the Ordre Pour le Mérite. Of course, my joy was tremendous.' (Library of Congress)

Von Richthofen is seen here in the centre of this group of pilots from his squadron. Lothar von Richthofen, Manfred's younger brother, is seen second from right and Kurt Wolff, another high-scoring ace, is on the right. (Phil Carradice Collection)

Another view of Lothar von Richthofen. Lothar was also an accomplished fighter pilot, and his score would have been higher had he not spent so much time in hospital. Despite that, he survived the war only to be killed in a crash while working as a commercial pilot. (Phil Carradice Collection)

Ernst Udet. With sixty-two victories, Udet was the second-highest-scoring German ace of the First World War, after Manfred von Richthofen. Udet would survive the war and serve in the Luftwaffe during the Second World War only to commit suicide on 17 November 1941. (Phil Carradice Collection)

Herman Göring, seen during his days as a fighter pilot with the Richthofen squadron. It was his service with Richthofen that made Göring a hero to many middle-class Germans and thus a useful propaganda asset for the Nazi Party. (Phil Carradice Collection)

A photograph of one of the German flying circuses, showing the tents which they used as hangars when they moved from place to place and a long line of multicoloured fighters. (John Christopher Collection)

English and French Flying
(February 1917)

I was trying to compete with Boelcke's squadron. Every evening we compared our bags. However, Boelcke's pupils are smart rascals. I cannot get ahead of them. The utmost one can do is to draw level with them. The Boelcke section has an advantage over my squadron of 100 aeroplanes downed. I must not allow them to retain it. Everything depends on whether we have for opponents those French tricksters or those daring rascals, the English. I prefer the English. Frequently, their daring can only be described as stupidity. In their eyes it may be pluck and daring.

The great thing in air fighting is that the decisive factor does not lie in trick flying but solely in the personal ability and energy of the aviator. A flying man may be able to loop and do all the stunts imaginable and yet he may not succeed in shooting down a single enemy. In my opinion the aggressive spirit is everything and that spirit is very strong in us Germans. Hence we shall always retain the domination of the air.

The French have a different character. They like to put traps and to attack their opponents unawares. That cannot easily be done in the air. Only a beginner can be caught and one cannot set traps because an aeroplane cannot hide itself. The invisible aeroplane has not yet been discovered. Sometimes, however, the Gaelic blood asserts itself. The Frenchmen will then attack. But the French attacking spirit is like bottled lemonade. It lacks tenacity.

The Englishmen, on the other hand, one notices that they are of Germanic blood. Sportsmen easily take to flying, and Englishmen see in flying nothing but a sport. They take a perfect delight in looping the loop, flying on their back, and indulging in other stunts for the benefit of our soldiers in the trenches. All these tricks may impress people who attend a sports meeting, but the public at the battlefront is not as appreciative of these things. It demands higher qualifications than trick flying. Therefore, the blood of English pilots will have to flow in streams.

SCOTLAND FOR EVER!

Gott strafe England, 'May God punish England', was one of the main German slogans of the
First World War. Manfred von Richthofen seems to have admired Britain and the British, but
of course many of his countrymen felt very differently, frustrated with the way it seemed that
Britain had blocked German colonial expansion and the way Britain had entered the war.
The Scottish soldier in this *Punch* cartoon, entitled 'Scotland For Ever!', has taken offence at
the slogan, but not perhaps in the way originally intended. (John Christopher Collection)

Two images of the French ace Charles Nungesser, showing him on his return from a flight (*above*) and taking off on another flight (*below*). 'The French ... like to put traps and attack their opponents unawares ... Sometimes, however, the Gaelic blood asserts itself. The Frenchmen will then attack. But the French attacking spirit is like bottled lemonade. It lacks tenacity.' (J&C McCutcheon Collection)

A group of British pilots pose in front of an aircraft. 'The Englishmen, on the other hand, one notices that they are of Germanic blood. Sportsmen easily take to flying, and Englishmen see in flying nothing but a sport … All these tricks may impress people who attend a sports meeting, but the public at the battlefront is not as appreciative of these things.' (J&C McCutcheon Collection)

A squadron of RFC monoplanes on an airfield somewhere in France. (J&C McCutcheon Collection)

A photograph of a British BE type, captured by the Germans. BE2s and BE12s feature among the list of Manfred von Richthofen's victories. (Library of Congress)

An SE5A fighter. The SE5, along with the Sopwith Camel, is one of the best-known British aircraft of the First World War, and also features on the list of von Richthofen's victories during 1917 and 1918. (J&C McCutcheon Collection)

I Am Shot Down
(Middle of March 1917)

I have had an experience which might perhaps be described as being shot down. At the same time, I call shot down only when one falls down. Today I got into trouble but I escaped with a whole skin.

I was flying with the squadron and noticed an opponent who also was flying in a squadron. It happened above the German artillery position in the neighbourhood of Lens. I had to fly quite a distance to get there. It tickles one's nerves to fly towards the enemy, especially when one can see him from a long distance and when several minutes must elapse before one can start fighting. I imagine that at such a moment my face turns a little pale, but unfortunately I have never had a mirror with me. I like that feeling, for it is a wonderful nerve stimulant. One observes the enemy from afar. One has recognised that his squadron is really an enemy formation. One counts the number of the hostile machines and considers whether the conditions are favourable or unfavourable. A factor of enormous importance is whether the wind forces me away from or towards our Front. For instance, I once shot down an Englishman. I fired the fatal shot above the English position. However, the wind was so strong that his machine came down close to the German captive balloons.

We Germans had five machines. Our opponents were three times as numerous. The English flew about like midges. It is not easy to disperse a swarm of machines which fly together in good order. It is impossible for a single machine to do it. It is extremely difficult for several aeroplanes, particularly if the difference in number is as great as it was in this case. However, one feels such a superiority over the enemy that one does not doubt of success for a moment.

The aggressive spirit, the offensive, is the chief thing everywhere in war, and the air is no exception. However, the enemy had the same idea. I noticed that at once. As soon as they observed us, they turned round and attacked us. Now we five had to look sharp. If one of them should fall there might be a lot of trouble for all of us. We went closer together and allowed the foreign gentlemen to approach us.

I watched whether one of the fellows would hurriedly take leave of his colleagues. There! One of them is stupid enough to depart alone. I can reach him and I say to myself, 'That man is lost.' Shouting aloud, I am after him. I have come up to him or at least am getting very near him. He starts shooting prematurely, which shows that he is nervous. So I say to myself, 'Go on shooting. You won't hit me.' He shot with a kind of ammunition which ignites, so I could see his shots passing me. I felt as if I were sitting in front of a gigantic watering pot. The sensation was not pleasant. Still, the English usually shoot with their beastly stuff, and so we must try and get accustomed to it. One can get accustomed to anything. At the moment, I think I laughed aloud. But soon I got a lesson. When I had approached the Englishman quite closely, when I had come to a distance of about 300 feet, I got ready for firing, aimed and gave a few trial shots. The machine guns were in order. The decision would be there before long. In my mind's eye I saw my enemy dropping.

My former excitement was gone. In such a position one thinks quite calmly and collectedly and weighs the probabilities of hitting and of being hit. Altogether, the fight itself is the least exciting part of the business as a rule. He who gets excited in fighting is sure to make mistakes. He will never get his enemy down. Besides, calmness is, after all, a matter of habit. At any rate, in this case I did not make a mistake. I approached my man up to 50 yards. Then I fired some well-aimed shots and thought that I was bound to be successful. That was my idea. But suddenly I heard a tremendous bang when I had scarcely fired ten cartridges. Presently, again something hit my machine. It became clear to me that I had been hit or rather my machine. At the same time I noticed a fearful benzine stench and I observed that the motor was running slack. The Englishman noticed it, too, for he started shooting with redoubled energy while I had to stop it.

I went right down. Instinctively, I switched off the engine and indeed it was high time to do this. When a pilot's benzine tank has been perforated, and when the infernal liquid is squirting around his legs, the danger of fire is very great. In front is an explosion engine of more than 150 hp which is red hot. If a single drop of benzine should fall on it, the whole machine would be in flames.

I left in the air a thin white cloud. I knew its meaning from my enemies. Its appearance is the first sign of a coming explosion. I was at an altitude of 9,000 feet and had to travel a long distance to get down. By the kindness of Providence, my engine stopped running. I have no idea with what rapidity I went downward. At any rate, the speed was so great that I could not put my head out of the machine without being pressed back by the rush of air.

Soon I lost sight of my enemy. I had only time to see what my four comrades were doing while I was dropping to the ground. They were still fighting. Their machine guns and those of their opponents could be heard. Suddenly I notice a rocket. Is it a signal of the enemy? No, it cannot be. The light is too great for a rocket. Evidently a machine is on fire. What machine? The burning machine looks exactly as if it were one of our own. No! Praise the Lord, it is one of the enemy's! Who can have shot him down? Immediately afterwards, a second machine drops out and falls perpendicularly to the ground, turning, turning, turning exactly as I did, but suddenly it recovers its balance. It flies straight towards me. It also is an Albatros. No doubt it had the same experience as I had.

I had fallen to an altitude of perhaps 1,000 feet and had to look out for a landing. Now, such a sudden landing usually leads to breakages and as these are occasionally serious, it was time to look out. I found a meadow. It was not very large but it would just suffice if I used due caution. Besides, it was favourably situated on the high road near Henin-Lietard. There I meant to land.

Everything went as desired and my first thought was, 'What has become of the other fellow?' He landed a few kilometres from the spot where I had come to the ground.

I had ample time to inspect the damage. My machine had been hit a number of times. The shot which caused me to give up the fight had gone through both benzine tanks. I had not a drop of benzine left and the engine itself had also been damaged by shots. It was a pity for it had worked so well.

I let my legs dangle out of the machine and probably made a very silly face. In a moment, I was surrounded by a large crowd of soldiers. Then came an officer. He was quite out of breath. He was terribly excited! No doubt something fearful had happened to him. He rushed towards me, gasped for air and asked, 'I hope that nothing has happened to you. I have followed the whole affair and am terribly excited! Good Lord, it looked awful!' I assured him that I felt quite well, jumped down from the side of my machine and introduced myself to him. Of course he did not understand a particle of my name. However, he invited me to go in his motor car to Henin-Lietard, where he was quartered. He was an Engineer Officer.

We were sitting in the motor and were commencing our ride. My host was still extraordinarily excited. Suddenly he jumped up and asked, 'Good Lord, but where is your chauffeur?' At first I did not quite understand what he meant. Probably I looked puzzled. Then it dawned upon me that he thought that I was the observer of a two-seater and that he asked after the fate of my pilot. I pulled myself together and said in the driest tones, 'I always drive myself.' Of course, the word 'drive' is absolutely taboo among the flying men.

An aviator does not drive, he flies. In the eyes of the kind gentleman I had obviously lost caste when he discovered that I 'drove' my own aeroplane. The conversation began to slacken.

We arrived in his quarters. I was still dressed in my dirty and oily leather jacket and had round my neck a thick wrap. On our journey he had of course asked me a tremendous number of questions. Altogether, he was far more excited than I was. When we got to his diggings he forced me to lie down on the sofa, or at least he tried to force me because, he argued, I was bound to be terribly done up through my fight. I assured him that this was not my first aerial battle but he did not, apparently, give me much credence. Probably I did not look very martial.

After we had been talking for some time he asked me of course the celebrated question, 'Have you ever brought down a machine?' As I said before, he had probably not understood my name. So I answered nonchalantly, 'Oh, yes! I have done so now and then.' He replied, 'Indeed! Perhaps you have shot down two?' I answered, 'No. Not two but twenty-four.' He smiled, repeated his question and gave me to understand that, when he was speaking about shooting down an aeroplane, he meant not shooting at an aeroplane but shooting into an aeroplane in such a manner that it would fall to the ground and remain there. I immediately assured him that I entirely shared his conception of the meaning of the words 'shooting down'.

Now I had completely lost caste with him. He was convinced that I was a fearful liar. He left me sitting where I was and told me that a meal would be served in an hour. If I liked, I could join in. I accepted his invitation and slept soundly for an hour. Then we went to the Officers' Club. Arrived at the club, I was glad to find that I was wearing the Ordre Pour le Mérite.

Unfortunately, I had no uniform jacket underneath my greasy leather coat but only a waistcoat. I apologised for being so badly dressed. Suddenly, my good chief discovered on me the Ordre Pour le Mérite. He was speechless with surprise and assured me that he did not know my name. I gave him my name once more. Now it seemed to dawn upon him that he had heard my name before. He feasted me with oysters and champagne and I did gloriously until at last my orderly arrived and fetched me with my car. I learned from him that comrade Lubbert had once more justified his nickname. He was generally called 'the bullet-catcher', for his machine suffered badly in every fight. Once, it was hit sixty-four times. Yet he had not been wounded. This time he had received a glancing shot on the chest and he was by this time in hospital. I flew his machine to port. Unfortunately this excellent officer, who promised to become another Boelcke, died a few weeks later – a hero's death for the Fatherland.

In the evening I could assure my kind host of Henin-Lietard that I had increased my 'bag' to twenty-five.

A biplane returning to its base after a mission, flying low over the front lines and no man's land. (J&C McCutcheon Collection)

A German pilot standing beside the wreckage of an aircraft. 'I have had an experience which might perhaps be described as being shot down. At the same time, I call shot down only when one falls down. Today I got into trouble but I escaped with a whole skin.' (J&C McCutcheon Collection)

A Flying Man's Adventure

The name 'Siegfried position' is probably known to every young man in Germany. During the time when we withdrew towards the Siegfried Line, the activity in the air was of course very great. We allowed our enemies to occupy the territory which we had evacuated but we did not allow them to occupy the air as well. The chaser squadron which Boelcke had trained looked after the English flying men. The English had hitherto fought a war of position in the air and they ventured to abandon it for a war of movement only with the utmost caution.

That was the time when Prince Frederick Charles gave his life for the Fatherland.

In the course of a hunting expedition of the Boelcke Chaser Squadron, Lieutenant Voss had defeated an Englishman in an aerial duel. He was forced to go down to the ground and landed in neutral territory between the lines, in No Man's Land. In this particular case, we had abandoned a stretch of territory but the enemy had not yet occupied it. Only English and German patrols were about in the unoccupied zone. The English flying machine was standing between the two lines. Our good Englishman probably believed that the ground was already in English possession and he was justified in thinking so.

Lieutenant Voss was of a different opinion. Without a moment's hesitation, he landed close to his victim. With great rapidity he transferred the Englishman's machine guns and other useful things to his own aeroplane, took a match and in a few minutes the English machine stood in flames. Then he waved smilingly from his victorious aeroplane to the English, who were rushing along from all sides, and was off.

Left: Werner Voss, reckless, dashing and brave, is seen here with von Richthofen. Killed in action in 1917, at the age of twenty, Voss would claim forty-eight victories. (Phil Carradice Collection)

Below: Prince Frederick Charles of Prussia setting out on his last flight in 1917. Von Richthofen's friend from the Lichterfelde academy was shot down on 21 March.

My First Double Event

2 April 1917 was a very warm day for my Squadron. From my quarters I could clearly hear the drumfire of the guns, which was again particularly violent.

I was still in bed when my orderly rushed into the room and exclaimed, 'Sir, the English are here!' Sleepy as I was, I looked out of the window and, really, there were my dear friends circling over the flying ground. I jumped out of my bed and into my clothes in a jiffy. My Red Bird had been pulled out and was ready for starting. My mechanics knew that I should probably not allow such a favourable moment to go by unutilised. Everything was ready. I snatched up my furs and then went off.

I was the last to start. My comrades were much nearer to the enemy. I feared that my prey would escape me, that I should have to look on from a distance while the others were fighting. Suddenly, one of the impertinent fellows tried to drop down upon me. I allowed him to come near and then we started a merry quadrille. Sometimes my opponent flew on his back and sometimes he did other tricks. He had a double-seated chaser. I was his master and very soon I recognised that he could not escape me.

During an interval in the fighting, I convinced myself that we were alone. It followed that the victory would accrue to he who was calmest, who shot best and who had the clearest brain in a moment of danger. After a short time I got him beneath me without seriously hurting him with my gun. We were at least 2 km from the front. I thought he intended to land but there I had made a mistake. Suddenly, when he was only a few yards above the ground, he once more went off on a straight course. He tried to escape me. That was too bad. I attacked him again and I went so low that I feared I should touch the roofs of the houses of the village beneath me. The Englishman defended himself up to the last moment. At the very end I felt that my engine had been hit. Still I did not let go. He had to fall. He rushed at full speed right into a block of houses.

There was little left to be done. This was once more a case of splendid daring. He defended himself to the last. However, in my opinion he showed more foolhardiness than courage. This was one of the cases where one must differentiate between energy and idiocy. He had to come down in any case but he paid for his stupidity with his life.

I was delighted with the performance of my red machine during its morning work and returned to our quarters. My comrades were still in the air and they were very surprised, when, as we met at breakfast, I told them that I had scored my thirty-second machine. A very young Lieutenant had 'bagged' his first aeroplane. We were all very merry and prepared everything for further battles. I then went and groomed myself. I had not had time to do it previously. I was visited by a dear friend, Lieutenant Voss of Boelcke's squadron. We chatted. Voss had downed on the previous day his twenty-third machine. He was next to me on the list and is at present my most redoubtable competitor.

When he started to fly home, I offered to accompany him part of the way. We went on a roundabout way over the fronts. The weather had turned so bad that we could not hope to find any more game.

Beneath us there were dense clouds. Voss did not know the country and he began to feel uncomfortable. When we passed above Arras I met my brother who also is in my squadron and who had lost his way. He joined us. Of course, he recognised me at once by the colour of my machine.

Suddenly we saw a squadron approaching from the other side. Immediately, the thought occurred to me, 'Now comes number thirty-three.' Although there were nine Englishmen and although they were on their own territory, they preferred to avoid battle. I thought that perhaps it would be better for me to repaint my machine. Nevertheless we caught them up. The important thing in aeroplanes is that they are speedy.

I was nearest to the enemy and attacked the man to the rear. To my greatest delight I noticed that he accepted battle and my pleasure was increased when I discovered that his comrades deserted him. So I had once more a single fight. It was a fight similar to the one which I had had in the morning. My opponent did not make matters easy for me. He knew the fighting business and it was particularly awkward for me that he was a good shot. To my great regret, that was quite clear to me.

A favourable wind came to my aid. It drove both of us into the German lines. My opponent discovered that the matter was not so simple as he had imagined. So he plunged and disappeared in a cloud. He had nearly saved himself.

I plunged after him and dropped out of the cloud and, as luck would have it, found myself close behind him. I fired and he fired without any tangible result. At last I hit him. I noticed a ribbon of white benzine vapour. He had to land for his engine had come to a stop.

He was a stubborn fellow. He was bound to recognise that he had lost the game. If he continued shooting I could kill him, for meanwhile we had dropped to an altitude of about 900 feet. However, the Englishman defended himself exactly as did his countryman in the morning. He fought until he landed. When he had come to the ground, I flew over him at an altitude of about 30 feet in order to ascertain whether I had killed him or not. What did the rascal do? He took his machine gun and shot holes into my machine.

Afterwards, Voss told me if that had happened to him he would have shot the airman on the ground. As a matter of fact, I ought to have done so for he had not surrendered. He was one of the few fortunate fellows who escaped with their lives.

I felt very merry, flew home and celebrated my thirty-third aeroplane.

A Bristol Fighter of the RFC. 'Sometimes my opponent flew on his back and sometimes he did other tricks. He had a double-seated chaser. I was his master and very soon I recognised that he could not escape me.' (Flickr/ San Diego Air and Space Museum)

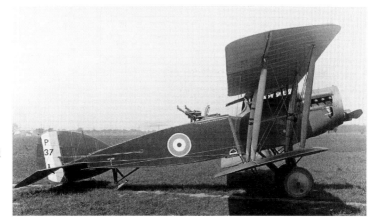

General von Hoeppner, commander of the German flying services, shaking hands with von Richthofen. (Phil Carradice Collection)

My Record Day

The weather was glorious. We were ready for starting. I had as a visitor a gentleman who had never seen a fight in the air or anything resembling it and he had just assured me that it would tremendously interest him to witness an aerial battle.

We climbed into our machines and laughed heartily at our visitor's eagerness. Friend Schäfer thought that we might give him some fun. We placed him before a telescope and off we went.

The day began well. We had scarcely flown to an altitude of 6,000 feet when an English squadron of five machines was seen coming our way. We attacked them by a rush as if we were cavalry and the hostile squadron lay destroyed on the ground. None of our men was even wounded. Of our enemies, three had plunged to the ground and two had come down in flames.

The good fellow down below was not a little surprised. He had imagined that the affair would look quite different, that it would be far more dramatic. He thought the whole encounter had looked quite harmless until suddenly some machines came falling down, looking like rockets. I have gradually become accustomed to seeing machines falling down, but I must say it impressed me very deeply when I saw the first Englishman fall and I have often seen the event again in my dreams.

As the day had begun so propitiously, we sat down and had a decent breakfast. All of us were as hungry as wolves. In the meantime, our machines were again made ready for starting. Fresh cartridges were got and then we went off again.

In the evening we could send off the proud report: 'Six German machines have destroyed thirteen hostile aeroplanes.' Boelcke's squadron had only once been able to make a similar report. At that time we had shot down eight machines. Today, one of us had brought low four of his opponents. The hero was a Lieutenant Wolff, a delicate-looking little fellow in whom nobody could have suspected a redoubtable hero. My brother had destroyed two, Schäfer two, Festner two and I three.

We went to bed in the evening, tremendously proud but also terribly tired. On the following day we read with noisy approval about our deeds of the previous day in the official communiqué. On the next day we downed eight hostile machines.

A very amusing thing occurred. One of the Englishmen whom we had shot down and whom we had made a prisoner was talking with us. Of course, he inquired after the Red Aeroplane. It is not unknown even among the troops in the trenches and is called by them 'le diable rouge'. In the squadron to which he belonged, there was a rumour that the Red Machine was occupied by a girl, by a kind of Jeanne d'Arc. He was intensely surprised when I assured him that the supposed girl was standing in front of him. He did not intend to make a joke. He was actually convinced that only a girl could sit in the extravagantly painted machine.

A German airfield seen from the air. (J&C McCutcheon Collection)

A very dashing artist's impression of an air raid by the RFC. (J&C McCutcheon Collection

The English Attack Our Aerodrome

Nights in which the full moon is shining are most suitable for night flying. During the full moon nights of the month of April, our English friends were particularly industrious. This was during the Battle of Arras. Probably they had found out that we had comfortably installed ourselves on a beautiful large flying ground at Douai.

One night, when we were in the Officers' Mess, the telephone started ringing and we were told, 'The English are coming.' There was a great hullabaloo. We had bombproof shelters. They had been got ready by our excellent Simon. Simon is our architect, surveyor and builder.

We dived down into shelter and we actually heard at first a very gentle humming and then the noise of engines. The searchlights had apparently got notice at the same time as we, for they started getting ready. The nearest enemy was still too far away to be attacked. We were colossally merry. The only thing we feared was that the English would not succeed in finding our aerodrome. To find some fixed spot at night is by no means easy. It was particularly difficult to find us because our aerodrome was not situated on an important highway or near water or a railway, by which one can be guided during one's flight at night. The Englishmen were apparently flying at a great altitude. At first they circled around our entire establishment. We began to think that they had given up and were looking for another objective. Suddenly we noticed that the nearest one had switched off his engine. So he was coming lower. Wolff said, 'Now the matter is becoming serious.'

We had two carbines and began shooting at the Englishman. We could not see him. Still, the noise of our shooting was a sedative to our nerves.

Suddenly he was taken up by the searchlights. There was shouting all over the flying ground. Our friend was sitting in a prehistoric packing case. We could clearly recognise the type. He was half a mile away from us and was flying straight towards us.

He went lower and lower. At last he had come down to an altitude of about 300 feet. Then he started his engine again and came straight towards the spot where we were standing. Wolff thought that he took an interest in the other side of our establishment and before long the first bomb fell and it was followed by a number of other missiles.

Our friend amused us with very pretty fireworks. They could have frightened only a coward. Broadly speaking, I find that bomb-throwing at night has only a moral effect. Those who are easily frightened are strongly affected when bombs fall at night. The others don't care.

We were much amused at the Englishman's performance and thought the English would come quite often on a visit. The flying piano dropped its bombs at last from an altitude of 150 feet. That was rather impertinent, for in a moonlit night I think I can hit a wild pig at 150 feet with a rifle. Why then should I not succeed in hitting the Englishman? It would have been a novelty to down an English airman from the ground. From above, I had already had the honour of downing a number of Englishmen, but I had never tried to tackle an aviator from below.

When the Englishman had gone we went back to mess and discussed among ourselves how we should receive the English should they pay us another visit on the following night. In the course of the next day our orderlies and other fellows were made to work with great energy. They had to ram into the ground piles, which were to be used as a foundation for machine guns during the coming night.

We went to the butts and tried the English machine guns which we had taken from the enemy, arranged the sights for night shooting and were very curious as to what was going to happen. I will not betray the number of our machine guns. Anyhow, they were to be sufficient for the purpose. Every one of my officers was armed with one.

We were again sitting at mess. Of course, we were discussing the problem of night fliers. Suddenly, an orderly rushed in shouting, 'They are there! They are there!' and disappeared in the next bombproof shelter in his scanty attire. We all rushed to our machine guns. Some of the men who were known to be good shots had also been given a machine gun. All the rest were provided with carbines. The whole squadron was armed to the teeth to give a warm reception to our kindly visitors. The first Englishman arrived, exactly as on the previous evening, at a very great altitude. He went then down to 150 feet and to our greatest joy began making for the place where our barracks were. He got into the glare of the searchlight.

When he was only 300 yards away someone fired the first shot and all the rest of us joined in. A rush of cavalry or of storming troops could not have been met more efficiently than the attack of that single impertinent individual flying at 150 feet.

Quick firing from many guns received him. Of course he could not hear the noise of the machine guns. The roar of his motor prevented that. However, he must have seen the flashes of our guns. Therefore I thought it tremendously plucky that our man did not swerve, but continued going straight ahead in accordance with his plan. At the moment he was perpendicularly above us, we jumped quickly into our bombproof shelter. It would have been too silly for flying men to die by a rotten bomb. As soon as he had passed over our heads, we rushed out again and fired after him with our machine guns and rifles. Friend Schäfer asserted that he had hit the man. Schäfer is quite a good shot. Still, in this case I did not believe him. Besides, every one of us had as good a chance at making a hit as he had.

We had achieved something, for the enemy had dropped his bombs rather aimlessly owing to our shooting. One of them, it is true, had exploded only a few yards from the 'petit rouge', but had not hurt him.

During the night the fun recommenced several times. I was already in bed, fast asleep, when I heard in a dream anti-aircraft firing. I woke up and discovered that the dream was reality. One of the Englishmen flew at so low an altitude over my habitation that in my fright I pulled the blanket over my head. The next moment I heard an incredible bang just outside my window. The panes had fallen a victim to the bomb. I rushed out of my room in my shirt in order to fire a few shots after him. They were firing from everywhere. Unfortunately, I had overslept my opportunity.

The next morning we were extremely surprised and delighted to discover that we had shot down from the ground no fewer than three Englishmen. They had landed not far from our aerodrome and had been made prisoners.

As a rule, we had hit the engines and had forced the airmen to come down on our side of the front. After all, Schäfer was possibly right in his assertion. At any rate, we were very well satisfied with our success. The English were distinctly less satisfied for they preferred avoiding our base. It was a pity that they gave us a wide berth, for they gave us lots of fun. Let us hope that they come back to us next month.

PUNCH, OR THE LONDON CHARIVARI.—July 18, 1917.

THE BUSINESS OF THE MOMENT.

John Bull. "I'VE LEARNED HOW TO DEAL WITH YOUR ZEPP BROTHER, AND NOW I'M GOING TO ATTEND TO YOU."

A cartoon from *Punch* showing the feeling that the Allies were now starting to gain the upper hand over the German fliers. (John Christopher Collection)

Right: Punch's take on the German bomber pilots. (John Christopher Collection)

Below: A Handley Page bomber. During the First World War, Handley Page built a series of bombers for the RFC and the RAF. 'Nights in which the full moon is shining are most suitable for night flying. During the full moon nights of the month of April, our English friends were particularly industrious … One night, when we were in the Officers' Mess, the telephone started ringing and we were told, "The English are coming." There was a great hullabaloo.' (Library of Congress)

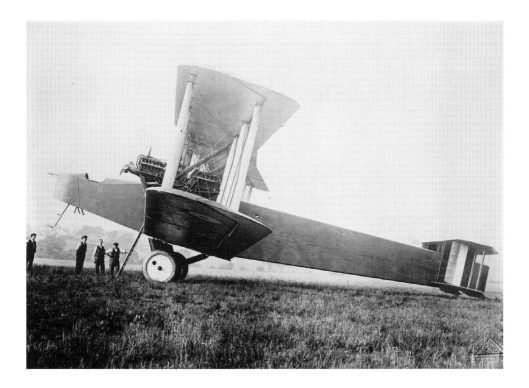

An image of an RFC bomber about to set off on a night raid. (J&C McCutcheon Collection)

In July 1917, Manfred von Richthofen was wounded in the head by a bullet in a fight over Ypres. Despite his anxiety to return to his unit, he was forced to spend time in hospital and in recuperation. This photograph shows a centre for treating wounded German officers. (J&C McCutcheon Collection)

When he was able to leave hospital, von Richthofen had to be accompanied by a nurse and there was speculation about a relationship between the two. (J&C McCutcheon Collection)

In the winter of 1917, Jasta 11 was re-equipped with the Fokker Triplane, the aircraft most associated in many people's minds with Manfred von Richthofen. However, the squadron was grounded over the winter of 1917/18 because of structural problems with the Triplanes. (John Christopher Collection)

The Sopwith Camel. Von Richthofen's last five victories were over Sopwith Camels. (Flickr/San Diego Air and Space Museum)

When von Richthofen was eventually shot down and killed, it was not by a fellow pilot; it was by a machine gun unit on the ground. (Library of Congress)

An artist's impression of a pilot dropping a wreath in tribute. When von Richthofen's death was confirmed, the RFC dropped a message of condolence to the base of Jasta 11. (J&C McCutcheon Collection)

Left: A photograph of a wreath dropped in condolence for the death of Max Immelmann. The war in the air was often seen as being more chivalric, and wreaths and condolences went across the lines. (J&C McCutcheon Collection)

Below: The Red Baron's funeral, conducted with full military honours by the nearest Allied flying unit to where he fell, No. 3 Squadron of the Australian Flying Corps. (John Christopher Collection)